PRAISE FOR ADRIAN SLYWOTZKY'S
THE ART OF PROFITABILITY

"Corporate strategy guru Adrian Slywotzky heeded his own much-published advice before he started his most recent book, *The Art of Profitability*: Study the customer."
—Boston Globe

"Reading *The Art of Profitability* is similar to patiently taking instruction from a martial arts sensei . . . without the physically punishing falls, that is."
—Industry Week Magazine

"Twenty-three agreeable—indeed, profitable—lessons."
—Harvard Magazine

"The book is written as a kind of Socratic dialogue between a world-wise profit guru and a young and promising executive. It is designed to get more people within organizations thinking about profit and the way it is created in their company."
—Toronto Globe and Mail

"Adrian Slywotzky's *The Art of Profitability* isn't exactly a business how-to. Instead, it's a novel, imparting business sense in the form of a fictional story."
—Southwest Airlines Spirit

"*The Art of Profitability* is an attractive and refreshing concept that taps into the Zen of business. Those seeking a new alternative to tired business manuals should revel in its main character's fable-like teachings."
—Publishers Weekly

"A complete toolbox of strategic models for profit making."
—Richmond Times-Dispatch

Also by Adrian Slywotzky

How to
GROW
When
MARKETS
DON'T

ADRIAN SLYWOTZKY
and RICHARD WISE
with Karl Weber

Published by Warner Books

An AOL Time Warner Company

Warner Business Books are published by Warner Books, Inc.,
1271 Avenue of the Americas, New York, NY 10020.

Visit our Web site at www.twbookmark.com

 An AOL Time Warner Company

The Warner Business Books logo is a trademark of Warner Books, Inc.

Printed in the United States of America

First Printing: April 2003
10 9 8 7 6 5 4 3 2 1

Library of Congress Cataloging-in-Publication Data

Slywotzky, Adrian J.
    How to grow when markets don't / Adrian Slywotzky and Richard
Wise with Karl Weber.
        p. cm.
    ISBN 0-446-53177-4
    1. Industrial management—United States. 2. Corporations—
United States—Growth—Case studies. I. Wise, Richard, II. Weber,
Karl, III. Title.

HD70.U5 S55 2003
658.4'06—dc21

                                                        2002191068

Book design by Giorgetta Bell McRee

Contents

PART ONE

A Different Way to Grow

1

The Growth Crisis

This is a book about growth—specifically, about how you can grow your business in the difficult environment most companies are facing now and will face in the decades to come.

Many businesspeople think of the postwar decades as a golden era of routine, almost reflexive growth. This picture is exaggerated but fundamentally accurate. It *was* significantly easier for most firms to rapidly and steadily increase their revenues and profits during those years than it is today. Many great companies were built using a model that appears, in retrospect, exceedingly simple: Invent a great product. Launch it. Sell it like hell. Go international. Acquire and consolidate. Cut costs. Raise prices if you can. Repeat ad infinitum.

But as most businesspeople realize, cracks have long been spreading in that traditional model of business growth.

The first major stress on this traditional growth

model came with the rise of the business design innovators beginning in the mid-1980s. Companies such as Southwest Airlines, Nucor, and Wal-Mart focused not on product innovation but on inventing new ways to better serve the customer, capture value, and create strategic control in their industries. They created innovative *business designs* even as they sold products similar to everyone else's.

The result was that billions of dollars of shareholder value migrated from the traditional industry leaders such as United Airlines, U.S. Steel, and Sears to these upstarts. We've learned a lot by studying the business design innovation methods developed by these companies and other industry leaders, and many of our consulting clients, as well as readers of our previous books, *Value Migration, The Profit Zone,* and *The Art of Profitability,* have benefited from applying the same ideas to their own businesses.

Within the past five years, though, we've begun to observe a new and troubling pattern. What was once value migration from one business model to another has increasingly changed into *value outflow.* Profits and shareholder value are leaving industries altogether as markets become increasingly saturated and traditional sources of growth run out of steam.

This value outflow points out a key challenge to business design innovators in today's marketplace. Most have done little to shape new customer needs beyond those addressed by traditional product offerings. Take Southwest Airlines, for instance. It has built an innovative point-to-point route system with lower overall costs than the major airlines, but it still sells only the standard airline seat. It hasn't redefined the travel experience or created new demand by helping customers in some special way before or after they occupy that seat. The same is true of Nucor in steel or Wal-Mart in general merchandise retailing or Dell in computers. All have successful but fundamentally product-focused business designs.

Out of Steam

Unfortunately, in the years to come, traditional product-centered strategies alone will be unable to create the kind of growth companies desire.

In the past, companies searching for growth opportunities have relied on classic product-focused growth strategies: Create innovative products, expand the market for them globally, and make acquisitions to gain market share and create efficiencies. These traditional growth moves are as important as ever (and for a few companies, even more important). But for most companies, these moves will merely replace revenues and profits lost to commoditization and increased competition. They won't represent a platform for driving significant, sustained new growth. This is true for a variety of reasons. Let's begin with the challenging dynamics facing product-innovation-oriented growth moves: brand extensions, core product enhancements, and new-product introductions.

After years of brand extensions, most spin-off

products are serving ever-smaller niche markets and fighting for space on increasingly crowded shelves. (The same applies to such basic services as banking, hospitality, and travel, which can be thought of as "products" in this context.) For example, between 1980 and 1998, the number of annual new food product introductions in the United States grew *five-fold,* to nearly eleven thousand. Similarly daunting statistics could be cited for cars and CDs, books and cosmetics, toys and televisions. In such an environment of saturation, is the world waiting eagerly for your next product extension? Not likely.

Thus, most companies' product extensions—think of American Express Optima or Pepsi Blue—are producing increasingly small returns in terms of growth, especially in percentage terms. The bigger your company, the bigger the growth opportunities you need if you hope to achieve double-digit growth. But while many of the billion-dollar companies of fifteen yeas ago had robust product extension pipelines, the same pipelines are producing only a trickle of growth for today's $10 billion companies. The disproportion is growing increasingly painful.

Product enhancement is another largely depleted avenue for new profit growth. In most industries, truly differentiating new-product breakthroughs are becoming increasingly rare. As a result, product competition in one industry after another is reduced to back-and-forth jockeying, as first one competitor and then another introduces a product with slightly better performance. Think of Nintendo and Sony, Intel and AMD, Boeing and Airbus, Avis and Hertz. The advantages gained in this tit-for-tat combat are invariably slender and fleeting.

And because meaningful product breakthroughs have become rare, customers are extending their product replacement cycles. If the newest car, copier, or computer is only marginally better than last year's model, customers can wait longer to replace it. Sales growth thus shrinks further.

Even new-product innovation is a largely depleted avenue for consistent profit growth. Of course, there will always be new technologies and new products, and some of these will provide genuine growth opportunities. But the intensity of today's product competition means that most product-driven growth is likely to be increasingly low-margin and short-lived. This is why consumer electronics companies struggle to post profits despite a never-ending cascade of new gadgets.

In high-tech industries, the vast majority of companies and initiatives founded on breakthrough technologies fail to get off the ground. Think of NeXT Computer, Apple's Newton, or Sprint's ION communications platform. Even the most successful high-tech companies have been "bottle rockets" that experience three to four years of spectacular growth and stellar financial performance followed by equally spectacular collapse, as newer technologies emerge and customer needs shift. This pattern has been borne out in the histories of such former high-fliers as Wang, Data General, Rolm, and Digital. Recently, with companies such as Lucent and Palm, this cycle has compressed to two years.

Thus, while technological innovation will be a source of growth for some companies and is clearly a major contributor to macroeconomic growth, relying on it for sustained growth is a highly risky proposition.

For all these reasons, the vast majority of companies are now finding that product innovation is, at best, a source of profit replacement or profit protection; it isn't a source of new, long-term growth.

The other legs of the traditional growth strategy, international expansion and acquisitions, are also largely depleted of their potential.

International markets, often viewed as a rich field for growth, have indeed created decades-long growth for companies such as Coke, Boeing, and McDonald's. Increasingly, however, international markets hold declining opportunities for significant new growth. For one thing, many companies have already exploited the richest international opportunities. A decade ago, international sales might have been 15 to 20 percent of revenues at most Fortune 500 companies. Today, foreign markets drive 40 to 50 percent of revenues. In addition, in most industries, the largest foreign markets—Western Europe and Japan—are now as mature, competitive, and saturated as the United States. And most emerging markets, despite all the billion-consumers-in-China rhetoric, are much smaller, especially when measured by consumer and industrial purchasing power rather than by mere head count. They're also generally plagued by inefficient distribution channels, economic and political instability, and protectionist laws.

Worse, emerging markets that once looked promising are increasingly producing world-class competitors that challenge U.S. firms not only abroad but also on their home turf (think of Korea's Samsung in electronics and Hyundai in autos). Or they backslide suddenly into economic chaos (think of Brazil, Argentina, Russia, and Thailand).

Now let's turn to mergers and acquisitions, a huge component of the 1990s growth story. From 1994 to 2000, M&A activity grew sevenfold to $1.4 trillion per year. But the pace of deal making has dropped precipitously as the high stock valuations that allowed many companies to make cheap acquisitions in recent years have dropped back to more reasonable levels. In many industries, moreover, consolidation has reduced the number of viable acquisition targets to a handful, making antitrust concerns a barrier to future growth through M&A. In any case, numerous studies have shown that acquisitions rarely produce new value and often lead to disaster, which has dampened investor enthusiasm for such moves.

When you strip away the effects of international expansion and merger activity from the seemingly impressive growth rates of the 1990s, what remains is often less than impressive. Many companies with nominal growth rates in the double digits have real growth rates in their base businesses of less than 5 percent. That holds true even without considering the use of aggressive and sometimes dubious accounting practices to boost reported revenues—a big problem and one that's much harder to disentangle.

The popularity of such practices is, at one level, a symptom of the spreading growth crisis.

Creating sustained growth is hard under the best of circumstances. From 1990 to 2000, just 7 percent of publicly traded companies in the U.S. enjoyed eight or more years of double-digit growth in revenues and operating profits. As the growth crisis worsens in the coming decade, you can expect this percentage to shrink significantly—unless companies rethink their approach to growth.[1]

The Human Costs of the Growth Crisis

This is not an abstract problem but rather a painful day-to-day reality. No matter what role you play in the world of business, the chances are good that you've already begun to personally feel some of the effects of the breakdown of the traditional growth model.

If you're a middle manager, for example, you've probably found yourself having thoughts like this:

Over the past few years, things have been getting tougher and tougher for me at work. I used to be able to glide from one success to the next. But lately, the raises have been getting smaller and the promotions less frequent. It keeps getting

[1]For more detailed discussion and analysis of the challenges facing the traditional growth model, please visit our website at www.DemandInnovation.com.

harder to win approval for new investments, new hiring, or new equipment.

When I first joined the company, it felt like an upbeat, innovative, forward-looking place. Now I'm not so sure. The top brass keep saying, at least in public, that this is just a cyclical downturn . . . that all we have to do is batten down the hatches and ride out the storm. But I don't think I believe that anymore.

I still have a job—knock on wood!—but who knows how long that'll last. When my company stock holdings soared back in the 1990s, I toyed with the idea of early retirement. But for the past three years, they've been sliding sideways at best, and now I wonder if I'll ever be able to stop working.

Worst of all, work just isn't much fun anymore. Walking down the hall, I used to hear laughter and lively debates. Now I hear people whispering nervously behind half-closed office doors. I used to look forward to Monday morning. Now I just try not to think about it.

If you're a senior executive, you silently share many of the grimmer feelings of the middle manager . . . along with a few special torments of your own:

It's always been tough to be a company leader. There's a lot on my shoulders—that's the nature of the job. But the weight sure feels heavier today than it did five years ago.

The problem is that earnings growth has gotten

so hard to come by. Everyone I pass in the hall-ways is looking to me for answers. They're counting on me, and I know it. At staff meetings, I look determined and promise that the initiatives we're undertaking will turn all the trend lines up. But how am I going to deliver?

We have a strategic planning team that dutifully prepares reports recommending new-growth initiatives. Trouble is, the last ten proposals I've read look like the same ideas our company tried three years ago and five years ago. They didn't work then, and they won't work now. I visit the folks in R&D. They're just as smart and diligent as ever. But the new-product concepts they're working on look small, tired, and unappealing. How are they supposed to usher in a new era of growth?

My job has always been tough, but it used to be fun, too. Now it seems I spend my days scrambling to meet earnings forecasts to keep the wolves of Wall Street at bay. We cut costs a little more here, accelerate revenues a little more there, push a little more inventory out to the retail level somewhere else. I feel as if I'm endlessly pulling rabbits out of hats. Worst of all, deep inside, I'm pretty sure that one day soon the miracles will come to an end, and there won't *be* any more rabbits to produce.

Even the professional investor or money manager, who makes a living by picking winners among the thousands of publicly traded companies, is suffering because of the growth crisis:

Not so long ago, it was easy to deliver double-digit returns to my clients. The challenge wasn't where to invest; it was where to get enough money to chase all the good ideas.

The world seemed to be full of opportunities. New markets were opening up around the world. New technologies were revolutionizing one industry after another. And for years, the markets behaved as if the old rules about P/E ratios and earnings yield had been repealed. The multiples soared, kids straight out of MIT or Stanford became millionaires, and every quarter my portfolio went up another 8 or 10 or 12 percent. Those were the days.

Now it seems to be almost impossible to find solid companies with meaningful growth plans. Most are pinning their hopes on tired old tactics that even they don't really seem to believe in. And after the dot-com collapse, the telecom fiasco, and the accounting scandals, I'm almost afraid to look at my Bloomberg screen. It seems like every other day, some company I believed in and supported with my investors' money comes out with a new round of bad news—an earnings restatement or massive layoffs or a CEO firing.

As for those fancy new economic models that no one can explain in one-syllable words, I don't even want to hear about them anymore.

The question I keep asking myself: *Where can I find companies to invest in that have **real** prospects for long-term growth?*

If you've had such thoughts or conversations, you may have assumed they were symptoms of some personal malaise or a problem affecting one company or one industry. In fact, they are symptoms of something much more profound. Companies looking for *significant, sustained* growth in the future will need to find new platforms for growth. Otherwise, their stock prices will be going nowhere, while their talent goes elsewhere.

The Great Divide

Maybe these kinds of complaints don't resonate with you. Maybe you and your company have avoided the growth crisis so far. If so, congratulations. You are in the distinct minority.

During the past decade, most companies have crossed a great divide, moving from a past of strong growth for their base businesses into a future of low or no growth. Many did so without fully recognizing the change. The crucial shift occurred at different times in different businesses.

For Polaroid, the moment might have been in 1992.

For McDonald's, in 1994.

For Gillette, in 1997.

For Hewlett-Packard, in 1999.

For Merck, it is just beginning.

What about your company? What are the prospects for product-based growth in your industry? Have you already passed over into the no-growth zone, or is the shift coming in the next year, or two, or five?

The timing is important, because a delay in recognizing the problem exacerbates it, sometimes fatally. It takes two to four years for an organization to learn how to create truly *new* growth. The sooner you acknowledge the problem and move to address it, the better your chances of beating it.

Demand Innovation

The good news is that we've recently begun to observe a new form of business design innovation—a new response to the challenge of growth that is being pioneered by a handful of farsighted companies. These companies are focused on creating new growth and new value by addressing the hassles and issues that *surround* the product rather than by improving the product itself. They have shifted their approach from product innovation to *demand innovation*.

Rather than being about value migration, demand innovation is about creating *new growth* by expanding the market's boundaries. It focuses on using one's product position as a starting point from which to do new things for customers that solve their biggest problems and improve their overall performance. Thus, companies skilled in demand innovation do more than simply take value and market share away from traditional businesses. They also create new value and new growth in revenues and profits, even in mature industries that appear to have reached a plateau.

We've written this book to explore the new art of demand innovation, as illustrated by the stories of several of today's most innovative growth companies, including Cardinal Health, Johnson Controls, Air Liquide, GM OnStar, John Deere Landscapes, and Clarke American. The names of these companies may not be as familiar to you as those of Southwest Airlines, Wal-Mart, Intel, Dell Computer, and the other practitioners of value migration. They compete in widely divergent industries, and the specific business strategies they practice vary greatly. But all have one thing in common: They have managed to create impressive new revenue and profit growth in industries or industry niches that most observers and business leaders consider inhospitable to growth.

The more we studied the approach to business practiced by Cardinal, Johnson, and the rest, the more convinced we became that it represented a genuinely new phenomenon. Like Dell, Wal-Mart, and the other masters of value migration, the new-growth innovators are great business model innovators as well as imaginative and insightful analysts of the business environment, skilled at recognizing opportunities where others do not and developing profitable ways to respond. But where value migration businesses focus on reallocating value by responding to preexisting demand, new-growth businesses focus on growing new value by discovering new forms of demand.

Because demand innovation involves a new and emerging set of skills, many businesspeople will find it challenging to understand and master. But it can be done. We see traditional product-centered companies across a wide range of industries beginning to discover and create new business spaces with growth opportunities that will last not months or quarters but years or decades. In the chapters that follow, you'll learn about these firms and see what you can do to bring the same kind of new growth to your company, no matter what business you're in.

2

Beating the Crisis: Cardinal Health

The Distribution Squeeze

As a whole, healthcare in the U.S. is a vibrant industry. Total healthcare spending was $1.3 trillion in 2000, representing 13 percent of GDP. The aging of the baby boomers, coupled with the steady flow of new medicines, procedures, and devices, should drive continued growth for decades to come. At the newest frontier, biotechnology is poised to become the first great new industry of the twenty-first century. And the marquee segment of healthcare, pharmaceutical manufacturing, continues to generate lush profit margins, often greater than 20 percent.

But even a great industry has its tough patches. Consider the plight of the wholesale drug distributor—the company that buys pills and sprays and capsules from their makers and puts them on the shelves of the local pharmacy or into the hands of the emergency room nurse.

Demand is not the problem. Throughout the 1990s, in fact, sales of prescription drugs rose by 10 to 15 percent a year. But profits are a different story. It's a classic case of big, powerful customers growing ever bigger, more powerful, and more demanding, while distributors struggle to differentiate themselves. As hospital groups, pharmacy chains, HMOs, and insurers consolidated over the past decade, they put the price squeeze on suppliers. To stay ahead of these demands, distributors have had to pursue cost efficiencies with extraordinary diligence. Ten years ago, the average *gross* margin for a drug distributor was around 10 percent. Today, it has fallen to 4 percent. Average net margins hover around 1 percent. Finding resources to invest in new growth is extremely difficult in this ultra-demanding environment. Imagine looking for money for expansion, acquisitions, research and development—not to mention shareholder dividends, staff salary increases, and executive bonuses—in that kind of cash trickle.

Worse still, by the mid-1990s, most distributors were running out of new ways to grow that might provide some relief from this price squeeze. The consolidation that swept the industry in the late 1980s and early '90s had run its course, leaving three major players in the game. And international expansion wasn't a real option, given the high degree of government supervision over the healthcare sector in most countries.

But in the past five years, Cardinal Health, one of the big three pharmaceutical distributors, has managed to uncover and capitalize on one new opportunity after another, turning its apparently tough market position into a remarkable platform for growth. Rather than limiting the firm to a low-value-added role, Cardinal's position as a leading pharmaceutical distributor has given it unique access to customers, the systems and know-how to help them manage their problems, and the flexibility to move effectively in several complementary directions. The result: a track record of continuous demand innovation that has created double-digit growth in revenues and operating profits, and more than $25 billion in market value creation over the past five years.

Defining the Customers' Biggest Problems

The seed of Cardinal's growth was the realization that the same intermediary position that subjected it to the distribution squeeze also offered the company a uniquely privileged vantage point from which to view and understand the economic challenges emerging in the healthcare industry.

As a pharmaceutical middleman, Cardinal could see, touch, talk to, and connect with every player in healthcare—hospitals, pharmacies, drug manufacturers, HMOs, and others. It had the opportunity to study firsthand the pressures that each of these groups confronted daily. It knew how their economics were changing and how their priorities were shifting as a result. Therefore, when Cardinal surveyed the healthcare industry in the mid-1990s, rather than seeing only the limitations of its own narrowly defined role, it saw a host of tough economical problems facing its customers, each representing a potential opportunity.

The first was controlling costs. The HMO revolution had compressed reimbursement rates for medical procedures. In addition, the government was trying to constrain healthcare inflation by limiting the amount that Medicare and Medicaid would pay for procedures. In combination, these efforts placed tremendous cost pressures on caregivers.

At the same time, hospitals were wrestling with talent shortages. Even as the demand for healthcare services grows, the talent pool to provide such services is shrinking. Between 1994 and 1999, applications to pharmacy schools fell by a third, and the average vacancy rate for pharmacists at U.S. hospitals currently hovers around 21 percent. Things are even worse in nursing: A shortage of 450,000 RNs is expected by 2008.

A third problem facing care providers was antiquated information management. Healthcare is the original knowledge-intensive industry. But in their information management methods, hospitals and other healthcare facilities have scarcely reached the twentieth century, to say nothing of the twenty-first. Just one example: *Handwritten* notes, orders, and prescriptions are still the most commonplace and important documents in the realm of patient care. Jokes about doctors' lousy handwriting don't amuse hospital administrators who face million-dollar lawsuits over medication errors.

Taken together, these three problems led to a common result for Cardinal's hospital customers: a rising level of tension between the need for cost reduction and the demand for high-quality patient care.

The crucial question for Cardinal in the mid-1990s: *How does this tension create opportunities for us to help the customers—while still making a profit?*

Follow the Pill

Cardinal's intermediary role gave the company more than simply a venue from which to observe its customers' problems. It also gave Cardinal the know-how and the customer access to make those problems its own.

Cardinal's first set of responses could be summed up in the phrase *follow the pill*. The company's distribution business already handled pharmaceutical distribution from the manufacturer to the healthcare provider. But there's another distribution chain *within* the hospital that traditional distributors didn't address. This internal chain includes physicians and other professionals who prescribe medications; hospital pharmacists and pharmacy technicians who count out and package the medications; nurses and technical workers who run satellite storage and dispensing systems in individual hospital units; the doctors and nurses who deliver the medications to the patients; and information specialists in the pharmacy, patient record, and administrative departments of the hospital.

Even when this complex chain works correctly, it's difficult and costly to staff and administer. And every step in the process introduces an opportunity for error and needless expense. Pills get lost or stolen; medication is administered in the wrong amount, at the wrong time, or not at all; potentially dangerous drug interactions are overlooked; records aren't properly updated; patients or insurers are charged too much or too little; and so on.

These problems are far from trivial. Consider the numbers associated with just one of them. Every year, some four billion prescriptions are filled for American patients. Less than one-tenth of 1 percent of them produce drug interactions serious enough to require hospitalization—but that number is 2.7 million. Less than 2 percent of these interactions are fatal—but the number of deaths is fifty thousand. That's more than the number of Americans killed annually in auto accidents.

Cardinal saw that following the pill could mean more than helping hospitals save a little time and money. It could also mean helping hospitals get a handle on the three troubling trends—cost pressures, talent shortages, and poor information management—that were plaguing them.

Cardinal was uniquely well positioned to do this. Because the company was already adept at handling, managing, and tracking drugs at the wholesale level, it was a logical step to deploy those skills *inside* its customers' organizations. Cardinal could leverage its existing information systems and distribution management expertise to address these issues more cheaply and effectively than hospitals could on their own. And because Cardinal already carried the drugs to the hospital door, it was in a natural position to make the next move into the hospital itself. In effect, Cardinal began pushing the boundary of its own operations into territory traditionally controlled by its customers.

For example, it began to offer logistics management services for hospital pharmacies, applying its superior systems to some of the hospitals' most burdensome tasks. Soon, Cardinal was providing complete pharmacy management services, including the systems, staff, and oversight needed to run a pharmacy. Both the company and its customers were winners: Cardinal enjoyed new streams of revenue and profit, and the hospitals were relieved of the challenge of staffing and managing their own pharmacies. Today, through its Owen Healthcare brand, Cardinal manages over four hundred hospital pharmacies, more than all of its competitors combined.

This was just the beginning. Cardinal's follow-the-pill approach led it much deeper into the hospital— all the way to the hallway outside the patient's room. To get there, Cardinal acquired Pyxis Corporation in 1996.

Pyxis was a small company that made machines that automated much of the drug administration process. Think of ATMs that dispense medicines instead of cash. A nurse keys patient data into the Pyxis MedStation box, and the machine accurately doles out premeasured, bar-coded doses of medication, ready for use. Pyxis enables Cardinal to bring new value to customers and extend its distribution role literally to the patient's bedside.

The first-generation Pyxis MedStation system was developed to control the use of narcotics, which make up some 20 percent of the drugs used in hospitals (and which are especially vulnerable to loss and theft). Secure handling of controlled substances is still an important benefit of the machines; in fact, the newest MedStations use finger scanning to keep unauthorized hands away from the drugs. The system also reduces medication errors and the time and energy demands on overworked nurses. With the MedStation providing bar-coded, presorted, individual pill packets, the job of administering medications several times a day to a unit full of patients becomes much faster, easier, and more accurate.

By itself, Pyxis would be merely a nice add-on service for Cardinal to offer its customers. But Cardinal realized it could do more. Linking its distribution processes to the information capabilities of Pyxis could produce economic magic:

- Pyxis could reduce the risk of dangerous drug interactions by automatically transferring drug administration data to patient records and monitoring the medications prescribed.
- Pyxis could improve the timeliness and accuracy of

billing by sending patient drug usage data directly to hospital billing systems.

- Pyxis could also reduce the capital and operating costs associated with pharmacy management by linking directly with Cardinal's distribution systems to automate portions of the ordering and inventory management process.

Today, Pyxis machines do all of these things. Not surprisingly, hospitals love the system. Inventories, errors, and costs are all lower.

Jerry Reed, director of the pharmacy at the Atlanta Medical Center, says, "Pyxis really improves patient safety. It's impossible for nurses to accidentally pull the wrong drug for a patient, which reduces our risk and liability for medical errors."

Don Pearson, staff pharmacist at St. Joseph Hospital and Health Care Center in Tacoma, Washington, says that before Pyxis, "about 75 percent of my time was spent on distribution issues, and any clinical work was continuously interrupted by people trying to get me to stop what I was doing to help them get a med." Today, "pharmacists working upstairs are free to pursue clinical services uninterrupted."

For Cardinal, Pyxis proved that doing more for the customer need not mean spending more on enhanced service while generating little incremental revenue. In fact, Pyxis augments the traditional slender profit margin from drug distribution with a healthy annuity revenue stream generated by leasing Pyxis systems to hospitals.

Today, Cardinal dominates the automated drug

dispensing market, serving about 90 percent of the hospitals that use such machines. The array of Pyxis offerings has expanded to include machines that dispense patient gowns, suturing kits, and other supplies. And since many hospital units in the U.S. have yet to automate, Pyxis has significant room to grow.

Growth at the Margin Enhances Growth at the Center

The Pyxis story also illustrates the positive feedback that can be created between new growth and the base business. Consider this question: What if a hospital likes the MedStation system but *doesn't* use Cardinal as its chief pharmaceutical distributor?

On one level, there's no problem. Pyxis works fine with competing distributors. But the system is optimized to work with Cardinal since the automatic reorder protocol is connected directly to the Cardinal warehouse. So if a hospital orders medications from another pharmaceutical distributor, such as AmeriSourceBergen or McKesson, the drugs arrive in bulk containers rather than prepackaged totes, and the pharmacist will have to spend part of the morning sorting, counting, and repackaging. It doesn't take very long for most pharmacists to start lobbying to use Cardinal instead. Deploying Pyxis to solve deeper customer problems actually helped strengthen Cardinal's base business even as it created new growth.

Cardinal has grown enormously over the past

decade by expanding beyond the parameters of its original distribution business. Whereas all of the company's earnings came from pharmaceutical distribution in 1991, only half came from pharmaceutical distribution, with the other half from new businesses in 2001.

But, as the Pyxis example shows, this doesn't mean that Cardinal has neglected its base business. Quite the contrary. The company continued making distribution acquisitions in the 1990s, and as its new array of services provides new forms of customer value, the base distribution business thrives and grows stronger. As a result, Cardinal's market share in distribution has expanded from 4 percent to 29 percent in 2001, creating a more powerful platform from which to launch new services.

Another Growth Path: Serving the Surgeon

Building on the success of Pyxis, Cardinal realized that what worked for pills could also work for surgical supplies. Distribution of medical-surgical supplies is Cardinal's second largest business, after pharmaceutical distribution. It produces $6 billion in sales annually—about 15 percent of the company's total revenues. This business accounts for more than a quarter of total earnings, which is impressive considering that most of the medical-surgical gear Cardinal sells is simple, inexpensive, low-tech stuff such as gauze, tape, gloves, sutures, and suction tubes, which are used once and thrown away.

If any business would seem vulnerable to death by commoditization, this is it. But Cardinal has made it into a fountain of value, profit, and growth by leveraging its insights into healthcare's cost and efficiency challenges. How can a company that sells plastic gloves help solve these problems? By providing procedure-based delivery systems—surgical supply kits customized for specific physicians and specific operations.

Here's how it works. The average surgical procedure requires some two hundred products, which vary with the procedure and the doctor's preferences. In the traditional system, thousands of different items must be shelved in hospital storerooms, handpicked before a procedure, and transported on a tray to the operating room. The process is expensive, time-consuming, and error-prone. Inventory costs are huge. And plenty of staff time is devoted just to straightening up the storerooms, keeping track of items, ordering supplies, throwing out materials that have spoiled, and so on.

Cardinal's customized supply kits change all that and help customers reduce costs. The company provides an online ordering tool that allows surgeons to walk through their procedures in advance, picking the equipment and supplies they prefer. Products from twenty-two hundred manufacturers are available, though Cardinal itself makes about a third of what it sells. The two hundred or so items needed for a particular operation—an arthroscopic knee repair, for example—are then shipped to the hospital on the morning of the procedure in a sterile kit organized in the precise sequence in which they will be used. Every item in the kit has been preselected by the physician to be exactly the right one for the procedure.

You can see the benefits of this system to Cardinal's customers. Hospitals love the convenience of the prepackaged kits, the reduction in inventory and warehousing costs, and the saving of staff time needed to pick and transport supplies. Doctors love the customization and the elimination of error and uncertainty. And Cardinal has the ability to bundle its otherwise undifferentiated gloves and gauze into unique kits that carry premium prices for the convenience they provide.

As with Pyxis, the added value Cardinal brings to the surgical supply process also enhances the company's overall position with its customers. After all, once the surgical staff at St. Luke's has taught the Cardinal ordering system about their supply preferences for all of their most frequent procedures, why would the hospital consider shifting distributors? To switch would mean forcing their doctors to start over again with a new (and maybe less reliable) supplier. No hospital wants to annoy and alienate its surgeons, who are one of its best revenue and profit sources and are famously outspoken.

Cardinal has learned that your customers will have less and less reason to turn to competitors the closer and deeper your connection to them becomes.

Pharmacy management, MedStation, and surgical-kit supplies are just three of the businesses that have grown out of Cardinal's close link to hundreds of hospital customers and the leverage provided by its unique value chain position. Cardinal has gone on to develop a series of other value-added offerings for its hospital and retail pharmacy customers including customized resizing of drug packages, distribution of specialty pharmaceuticals and blood plasma, nuclear medicine applications, a branded retail pharmacy program, temporary staffing programs, supply chain optimization services, information technology tools for inventory and supply chain management, and consulting services.

Recognizing Upstream Opportunities

As a middleman, one of the most important groups Cardinal does business with operates upstream from it—the pharmaceutical companies. One of the ways Cardinal expanded its growth opportunities was by viewing pharmaceutical manufacturers not merely as suppliers but also as potential customers.

In the mid-1990s—when Cardinal began asking, How is the world of healthcare changing?—it recognized a major trend influencing the pharmaceutical industry: the increasingly demanding economics of the industry's blockbuster business model.

Pharmaceutical companies, like movie studios, record producers, and book publishers, rely on hit products to fuel their growth—in their case, blockbuster medications that can generate $1 billion or more in revenue annually. It takes years of research and thousands of failed experiments to develop a single blockbuster drug, which then must run a complicated gauntlet of tests and additional research to win regulatory approval, which usually takes several more years. And even after their initial release, most drugs with blockbuster potential take several years to grow to the billion-dollar sales level.

Meanwhile, every year some of the existing blockbusters that fuel the industry go off patent, opening the way for cheaper generic versions and effectively killing the golden egg. As a result, pharmaceutical firms are desperate to plow as much money, time, and energy as possible into their most critical pipeline-feeding activities, including drug discovery and clinical research, navigating the approval process, and marketing at both the professional and consumer levels. To free up capital and other resources for research, some firms are already seeking opportunities to divest themselves of their other operations; more will do so soon.

Cardinal realized that it could provide significant new value to pharmaceutical manufacturers by offering high-quality services in drug formulation, testing, manufacturing, and packaging, thereby freeing those firms to concentrate on the discovery and development of blockbusters.

Once again, Cardinal's role as a drug distributor gave the company advantages in pursuing the opportunity. As a distributor, it could bring efficiency and customer access to the pharmaceutical manufacturing business. Cardinal had a broad distribution reach, which would enable it to efficiently aggregate production and packaging volumes from multiple manufacturers. It had built important customer relationships, enabling access to high-level executives at the leading pharmaceutical manufacturers. It also had prior experience with custom packaging of drug products for its hospital and Pyxis customers as well as a track record of operational excellence and efficiency.

Building the Asset Base

To take advantage of this new upstream opportunity, Cardinal made use of a tactic that had served the company well in executing its downstream strategy: It supplemented its core assets with thoughtful acquisitions to deepen its technical and manufacturing capabilities.

Cardinal's upstream acquisitions have focused on buying companies in the drug formulation, manufacturing, packaging, and testing businesses. In doing so, the company has focused on value-added areas of the pharmaceutical industry and has avoided rapidly commoditizing areas such as simple manufacturing of basic pill forms. After making each purchase, Cardinal has moved quickly to reshape the acquired company so that it fits into Cardinal's vision of the future.

Consider RP Scherer, a drug delivery and contract

manufacturing firm that Cardinal purchased in 1998. Scherer was a solid company, but it lacked several of the assets it needed to grow quickly in the years ahead, including capital for investment and strong relationships with senior leadership at the top pharmaceutical firms—assets that Cardinal possessed. It also suffered from a lack of focus, deriving much of its revenue from the manufacturing of vitamins, nutritional supplements, and other near-commodity products.

Following the acquisition, Cardinal repositioned the company squarely in the pharmaceutical space. It sold Scherer's supplements and vitamins business, and it divested all of its nonpharmaceutical manufacturing plants. It also provided the expansion capital Scherer needed and, through its own network of relationships with the pharma companies, strengthened Scherer's ability to sell sophisticated drug design and manufacturing concepts. Today, fifteen of the top twenty pharmaceutical firms use Scherer to help them develop new forms for their drugs, and a dozen of the top one hundred blockbusters, from Schering Plough's Claritin to Eli Lilly's Zyprexa, are manufactured using Scherer technologies.

Not all of Cardinal's upstream growth moves are based on acquisitions. The company is internally building a new business in drug development and testing services—another set of functions that the pharmaceutical firms need help with. Cardinal has invested $80 million to create a product development and testing center in New Jersey. It now has the capability to take a newly discovered drug compound from formulation through testing, manufacturing, packaging, and final distribution, as well as provide sales and marketing services for small biotech and drug firms that lack those capabilities.

How Growth Begets Growth

As we've seen, Cardinal has been successful in creating new value both upstream and downstream from its original business. Now the company is beginning to link these positions to trigger a self-reinforcing cycle in which growth moves create more opportunities for growth through creative connections and integration.

Here's an example. Cardinal's downstream drug chain customers are dependent on third-party payments for most of the prescriptions they fill. Traditionally, these reimbursement rates are updated monthly in the payment systems. However, this often leaves money on the table for the chains because they miss recent rate increases; one study estimated this loss at fifty cents for each prescription.

To help ensure accurate payments, Cardinal worked with a number of the leading drugstore chains to develop a system called ScriptLINE, which automates the reimbursement process for pharmacies and updates rates daily. Now Cardinal not only supplies pharmaceuticals via its traditional distribution business but has also become a critical economic partner for the pharmacies by helping to set up a revenue collection system as well.

Even more powerfully, Cardinal is taking the data processed by ScriptLINE upstream to its pharmaceutical company customers through a new initiative known as ArcLight. A joint venture among Cardinal, Wal-Mart, CVS, Albertson's, and other retailers, ArcLight takes the sales information captured by ScriptLINE and repackages it for sale to pharmaceutical companies as timely market intelligence about what products are selling where—critical information given the money riding on getting blockbusters to market fast and effectively. Today, ArcLight customers include thirteen pharmaceutical manufacturers, and ArcLight data covers about one billion prescriptions per year—both figures that are expected to grow. A competing company called IMS Health has already built a billion-dollar business with a market capitalization of $5 billion providing such data. IMS collects its data through more traditional means such as retailer and doctor surveys, and it is typically a month old when released to clients.

As the creation of ArcLight illustrates, Cardinal's growth has been driven not by any single initiative but by many carefully sequenced moves that continuously open new growth paths, creating an ever-expanding set of opportunities for cross-pollination and value creation. In fact, CEO Walter goes so far as to say, "The breadth of our offerings is the core of our strategy."

The diversity of Cardinal's revenue streams also reduces the risk associated with any one source of income. This creates deeper, richer customer connections as well, since it multiplies points of contact and opportunities for Cardinal to observe, study, and understand the needs of its customers. As a result, the company's definition of its customer has expanded significantly from pharmacy purchasing agents to include pharmacists, doctors, hospital administrators, and pharmaceutical executives.

Jim Millar, president and chief operating officer in charge of Cardinal's pharmaceutical distribution and medical-surgical businesses, describes the growth opportunities in terms of customer "touches": "Wherever there's a touch, there's opportunity. It's one of the advantages of our diversified business portfolio. If we were just a drug distributor, we probably couldn't get in to talk to the guy in charge. But since we have a larger package to sell, we have another door we can knock on and another avenue for new business."

Paths Not Taken

It retrospect, we can see clearly how Cardinal's growth moves over the past seven years have unfolded logically from its initial middleman position. But it was not so obvious in the mid-1990s. If it had been, other companies would have made similar moves—or even preempted Cardinal.

It wasn't that other distributors didn't try to make growth-fueling moves. Some did. For example,

McKesson, Cardinal's largest competitor, spent $14 billion in 1998 to buy HBOC, a major supplier of enterprise software to hospitals.

On its surface, this was not a crazy gambit. Like Cardinal, McKesson was trying to expand its service offerings to one of its biggest customer groups—hospitals. Yet the acquisition has proven to be a financial and strategic failure. HBOC's software business, which was already slumping, has continued to decline, and any expected synergies have failed to materialize. What's the explanation?

Unlike Cardinal's acquisitions, McKesson's big play did little to leverage its existing assets—especially its network of links to hospital pharmacists. Instead, the company tried to make a giant leap to an entirely new marketplace—the hospital administrators and information technology experts who purchase enterprise software. In that arena, McKesson's preexisting relationships or distribution expertise could do little to raise the odds of success.

The HBOC acquisition wasn't necessarily a bad move for McKesson, but it was a bad *first* move. By contrast, we can appreciate how carefully the order of Cardinal's moves was planned. Cardinal went downstream first in a series of moves that allowed it to gather new information about those downstream customers and their pharmaceutical needs—favored doses, package sizes, trends in procurement, and so on. This knowledge was then used to help differentiate the company's offerings to its upstream customers. The *sequence* of Cardinal's moves was in many ways just as important as the moves themselves.

Big and Still Growing

From 1991 through 2001, Cardinal's compounded annual rate of revenue growth has been 40 percent, double that of its nearest competitor in the pharmaceutical distribution business. Operating profit growth has run at 42 percent, over three times the nearest competitor. Market value growth has run at 49 percent, more than double the nearest competitor. Cardinal now has annual revenues approaching $50 billion and ranks number 23 on the Fortune 500. As the business has expanded, its balance sheet has grown stronger. Debt is down while cash flow is up.

Cardinal is disproving one of the natural assumptions most business strategists make—that the bigger you are, the more difficult it is to find and seize growth opportunities. In fact, the Cardinal story illustrates that a big company can enjoy growth advantages that small companies lack—including a broad array of hidden assets, diverse income streams, pools of resources that can be used to fund growth, the ability to make new connections among customers and businesses, and a rich web of customer relationships. In combination, these advantages enhance Cardinal's ability to develop multiple growth paths from its central value chain position.

After a decade of remarkable growth, Cardinal continues to use, refine, and extend its growth system. It is also preparing for its next major challenge, that of growing a $50 billion company. Cardinal knows that the formula to reach $100 billion will not be the same one that got it to $50 billion, but it has built a broad and varied asset base that will give it several advantages in figuring out what that next formula will be.

3

Demand Innovation:
The First Half of Success

Next-Generation Demand

The Cardinal Health story is a powerful example of demand innovation in action. To achieve its remarkable growth, Cardinal found opportunities in a seemingly unpromising business landscape by identifying and serving a series of new customer needs, all focused on the activities that *surround* the products Cardinal sells.

Cardinal is rare, but not unique. In studying companies and industries over the past decade, we've come to recognize this as a typical pattern among those few companies that are most consistently successful at growth. These companies understand and exploit a little-noted truth: *While the product sale may be the culmination of the manufacturers' efforts, it usually marks the beginning of the customer's.*

Think about your own product or service. If your business is typical, your customers spend time, effort, and money figuring out how to use your product, maintain it, finance it, store it, and eventually dispose of it. It may have complex interactions with other products or be used as one input to a complicated process. It may serve more than one user, each with different needs and priorities.

We call this broader web of activity the customer's *internal value chain*. Embedded within it are all kinds of hassles and inefficiencies waiting to be improved, and it represents tremendous economic activity, often ten to twenty times greater in total value than the product market itself. Understanding and participating in this customer value chain is the key to demand innovation.

Recognizing Next-Generation Demand

What exactly do these customer value chain opportunities look like?

They begin with opportunities to support the customer through follow-on services such as installation, maintenance, financing, training, and outsourced operation. No company has exploited these opportunities more successfully than General Electric, which has leveraged its leading position in supplying such products as turbines, locomotives, and jet engines to provide lucrative downstream services that now account for up to 60 percent of GE's revenues and earnings.

The GE downstream services model is a powerful

one, but today's new-growth opportunities go well beyond this.

For example, there are significant opportunities to grow by helping customers *improve their cost structure,* reducing waste, excess operating and capital costs, and process inefficiencies. We've seen how Cardinal Health has opened up vast new opportunities in the healthcare industry by recognizing and addressing the inefficiencies associated with ordering, delivering, and dispensing drugs in hospitals and other settings. Similar opportunities exist in many other industries.

Often opportunities come from helping customers *reduce complexity, make better decisions, and speed their own offerings to market.* Auto parts maker Johnson Controls (see chapter 8) expanded its focus from the seat assembly market to the automotive interior market by taking on seat design and integration activities that traditionally had been performed by the carmakers themselves. The result for carmakers: better interior systems, lower capital requirements, faster design cycles, and lower overall costs. The result for Johnson: higher margins and broader access to the $85 billion market for car interiors.

An even more valuable benefit to customers can be helping them *reduce the risk and volatility* inherent in their business. Industrial gas provider Air Liquide (chapter 9) has created new revenue streams and profits by expanding beyond the industrial gas market into the much larger realm of manufacturing value-added. For one food manufacturer, Air Liquide set up and now runs the production line that finishes and freezes frozen omelets, taking on all responsibility for quality control, uptime, and throughput.

Perhaps the most valuable thing you can do for customers is help them *grow their top-line revenues.* Equipment maker John Deere (chapter 7) expanded its role in serving the needs of landscaping professionals through a new distribution business called John Deere Landscapes (JDL). One of its breakthrough offers is low-cost credit to its customers' customers through John Deere Finance, allowing them to spend more money on bigger and more elaborate landscaping projects. Check printer Clarke American (chapter 6) has developed innovative programs that help banks and credit unions retain their customers and sell them more lucrative financial services.

The Power of Next-Generation Demand

By offering their customers economic benefits beyond the functionality of their traditional products, all these companies have connected their products to bigger issues and bigger opportunities. In each case, they opened up greater market space and moved from a world where future growth expectations were measured in months or quarters to one with growth expectations measured in years or decades. They did so by using demand innovation to uncover three sources of new growth.

First, the focus on the next-generation demand

creates new, more powerful opportunities to grow core product sales by reinforcing and deepening customer relationships and shifting the basis of competition from product price and performance to new, more differentiated and valuable dimensions. Companies that play this game right capture a larger share of the customer's spending, enjoy better pricing, and often earn higher margins than their product-focused competitors. When Air Liquide manages the omelet line, it is pulling through associated gas sales based on the unique manufacturing expertise it can deliver rather than on traditional price and quality terms.

Second, by focusing on broader customer needs, the demand innovators are often able to *combine multiple products and services into more valuable integrated offers.* This allows them to capture new sales from adjacent markets and create a more lucrative balance between product and service sales. For John Deere, providing financing to its landscapers allows it to capture new, recurring revenues while also gaining the majority of their plant and irrigation spending.

Finally, a focus on next-generation demand offers opportunities to create entirely new avenues of growth by *turning the improvements in the customer's value chain into new revenue streams* from outsourcing fees, tolling charges, output guarantees, subscription fees, and the like. This happens when Cardinal charges a monthly fee for its Pyxis drug dispensing system based on the savings it brings to the hospital.

The best growth practitioners create growth along all three dimensions simultaneously. As a result, they create high-intensity profit growth in otherwise low-margin industries, enhance earnings stability, and forge tighter bonds with their customers. These benefits are compounded by the fact that new demand often begets new demand. Serving one set of customer needs often uncovers a new set.

Viewing Your Customer Through an Economic Lens

Demand innovation is about understanding and acting on your customers' most urgent problems and priorities by asking: *What are the issues they wrestle with every day? What are the headaches that keep them awake at night? How do their lives really unfold, both on and off the job? How do they spend their time, energy, and resources?* If you can answer questions like these, you will be able to define where you can do more to meet the new needs of customers, whether those customers are businesses or end consumers.

Unfortunately, most companies can't answer these questions, because they view their customers solely in terms of product needs. The secret to this richer opportunity of altering the customers' value chain lies in viewing customer activities through an economic lens. This means studying your customers' activities, costs, capital needs, information flows, and priorities. It means looking for bottlenecks, repetition, information gaps, and missed opportunities in your customer's processes that you can help alleviate or eliminate.

Viewing your customers through an economic lens can help you see what's *really* important to them, where the points of pain are in their internal value chain. This is something most customers can't articulate directly; next-generation needs are often so profound and ambiguous that customers haven't yet pinpointed them or put them into words. If you succeed in viewing and understanding your customers through an economic lens, you'll find in time that you've made an important shift—from *responding* to customer needs to *anticipating* them.

Redefining the Customer

Understanding your customers' most pressing issues is one part of the process of demand innovation. An equally important step is finding or developing a ready buyer for your proposed new offering. Often this is someone different from the traditional buyer of your product. Developing this new buyer is critical, because the old equation holds:

$$\text{Needs} - \text{Buyer} = \text{Zero}$$

As you shift your focus from providing product functionality to addressing more complex issues, you may need to move higher in the organization and earlier in the customer activity chain to find the right buyer. For instance, Air Liquide used to sell its commodity gases to a purchasing manager low in the hierarchy. By contrast, the buyer for a guaranteed output program such as the one with the omelet maker might be the plant general manager or business unit head.

Furthermore, as the identity of the decision maker changes, the complexity and intensity of the customer relationship will increase. The ultimate goal: to transform yourself from just another supplier into a key economic partner for your customer.

Consumers Have Needs, Too

So far, the examples we've cited have focused on the business-to-business marketplace. But next-generation needs abound in consumer markets as well. Some of today's smartest consumer companies are already moving to focus on such needs.

Consider Home Depot Expo, a store that brings together under one roof all of the major products and services involved in a home remodeling project. The store offers consumers a single, integrated source for flooring, lighting, kitchen and bathroom fixtures and cabinets, appliances and electronics, curtains, and accent items and furnishings, combined with seamless service for the entire project, from design and financing to construction and installation. Thus, Home Depot Expo cuts shopping time, streamlines the project planning process, and improves the quality of the finished work by ensuring that all the products chosen will fit together physically and aesthetically. The positive impact on consumers' time-and-hassle economics is profound. At the same time, the new business creates a powerful role for Home Depot at the center of the $150 billion home remodeling market.

At the experiential end of the spectrum, think about how Harley-Davidson expanded its business beyond motorcycles to offer a wide range of branded products and services, from specialized financing and rider rallies to motorcycle magazines, high-margin accessories and parts, logo-emblazoned jackets and gear, and upscale custom cycles. These offerings address customers' desire to celebrate their membership in a user community for whom the Harley lifestyle represents the freedom of the open road.

Just as in the business market, a shift in focus to next-generation demand gives consumer companies a more effective basis for differentiation, a stronger relationship with their customers, and valuable new nonproduct sources of value capture.

Making Demand Innovation Profitable

Demand innovation is difficult. One prerequisite is great performance in your core business. Only a company with world-class products and services has the credibility and authority to play in the demand innovation arena. So if your base business is hobbled by poor quality or inefficiency, that's the first thing you must remedy.

It's also essential that a great customer offering be supported by a viable *business design*. Solving a customer's deepest problem is valueless (in fact, it can be value-destroying) if the solution is not linked to a specific, accessible target buyer, a robust value-capture mechanism, and a clear source of competitive advantage.

Fortunately, there is a way to boost the odds of success and create high-profit demand innovation. The key lies in identifying and mobilizing a set of powerful hidden assets that your company has developed over the last two decades and whose existence you may scarcely recognize. In the next chapter, we'll examine these hidden assets, which are the last crucial elements in the equation for new growth.

4

Hidden Assets: Making a Good Opportunity Great

The Failure of "Providing Solutions"

Demand innovation is a promising answer to the growth crisis facing most companies. But identifying opportunities to address next-generation needs is only the first challenge. Equally important is the next question: *How can your company address these needs profitably?* After all, it's one thing to provide customers with new offerings that improve *their* economics; it's quite another to do so in a way that generates significant new value for *your* company.

The difficulty of both improving your customers' economics and capturing value for your company is a major reason for the failure of "providing solutions," one of the most widespread business clichés of the past few years. The concept of selling solutions isn't wrong. It's based on a valid recognition of the enormous unmet needs most customers have. But very few companies have figured out how to implement the concept profitably.

Most failed attempts to deliver solutions have suffered from one of two common flaws. First, many are uncompelling or undifferentiated in the customer's eyes. Sometimes the word *solution* is simply code for a consultative selling process or an attempt to pitch some kind of service agreement along with the product. Sometimes the solution is more significant, but undifferentiated. Take outsourcing as an example. Many companies have moved to take over and run some customer function, such as the mail room or call center, and then struggled to make money. The reason: In most cases, this is simply a cost-of-capital or -labor play, based on the notion that the contractor can run the operation more cheaply than the client firm. The function's role in enhancing the customer's business scarcely changes. Not surprisingly, this purely cost-based value proposition leads to rapid downward pricing pressure and service commoditization.

The other major problem with many attempts to create solutions is their complexity. Once a company has developed a compelling solutions offering, reaching and serving the customer often requires the creation of a highly skilled delivery force that is hard to scale up. The result is a small, marginally profitable operation that clings to relevance on the periphery of the business.

Hidden Assets—The Missing Puzzle Piece

But the notion of solutions needn't be an empty one. Cardinal and the handful of other companies we discussed in chapter 3 are redefining demand so as to improve their customers' economics *and* doing so profitably, turning the challenge into an opportunity for real, sustained growth. The secret is that they're using what we call *hidden assets* to turn marginal opportunities into great ones.

Here's the great news for established firms. As a by-product of doing business over several years or decades, virtually all established companies have developed pools of hidden assets with a potential value of billions of dollars. Yet these assets are ignored by most companies, especially in the context of the quest for growth.

In the coming battle to create next-generation growth, hidden assets will play a decisive role. When skillfully used, hidden assets can drastically reduce the cost of acquiring customers, the cost of developing unique offerings to address new customer needs, and the cost of delivering those offerings. In fact, the superior business economics enabled by the deployment of hidden assets can make the difference between an unprofitable new business and a profitable one, and between good and great investment returns.

Hidden assets are the missing puzzle piece that was overlooked in formulating the solutions concept. They are the key to *profitable* demand innovation.

The Power of Hidden Assets

You may be thinking *Hidden assets? Is that the same as **intangible assets**? Is this idea just old wine in a new bottle?*

Not at all. In recent years, there's been a lot of talk in business circles about intangible assets. But the discussion has centered almost entirely on three types: brands, competencies, and intellectual property. These are important, but the real universe of hidden assets is much broader, richer, and more powerful.

Furthermore, most analyses of intangible assets have focused on how to *value* these assets rather than how to creatively *deploy* them to create new growth. It's an interesting exercise in accounting theory, but it overlooks the real significance of your hidden assets. *The focus should be on connecting the hidden assets your company has developed to the next-generation demands of your customers.* If you make this connection, the value of your hidden assets will be enormous; if not, it will scarcely be worth measuring.

Learning to mobilize your hidden assets begins with a new way of looking at your company and its balance sheet. The traditional financial perspective assumes a narrow definition of company assets: factory, equipment, real estate, and money in the bank are the assets recognized on a balance sheet. If your approach is a bit more sophisticated, you may also acknowledge the value of your company's brands or people, although you probably have no precise way of quantifying this. The traditional definition of company assets generally stops here.

Now it's time to adopt a new perspective. Putting aside the financial lens, frame the issue from an entrepreneurial perspective. Ask yourself: *What assets beyond the traditional financial ones does my company own that an entrepreneur would love to have in order to create new value for customers?*

Chances are good that you own a number of hidden assets that any entrepreneur would envy. They may include *unique customer access, technical know-how, an installed base of equipment, a window on the market, a network of relationships, by-product information, or a loyal user community.* These and other hidden assets can be crucial in pursuing new growth because, if used skillfully and creatively, they can significantly improve the economics of meeting next-generation customer needs.

Let's look at a couple of examples to illustrate the dollar-and-cents value of hidden assets.

Suppose you want to build a new information business, perhaps selling services to help companies manage their software applications. Your target buyer is the chief information officer (CIO) of any large company. The question is: If you phone one hundred CIOs, how many of them will return your call the same day? If you are IBM, the answer is one hundred. If you are a start-up company, the answer is zero. The difference translates into months of delay in the customer acquisition process, lost or delayed revenues, and sharply reduced profits. That difference is the dollar value of the hidden asset called *customer access.*

Or consider one of the demand innovation examples cited in the last chapter. Suppose you want to build a business managing important food processing activities for customers from a standing start. How much time and money will you have to invest to gain the required expertise? How much will it cost for you to maintain employees on-site at the food plant? How long will it take you to build enough credibility so that a customer will allow you to run a critical section of its production line?

As a start-up, you can never hope to compete effectively with a company such as Air Liquide. Its experience, customer presence, and industry authority give it tremendous advantages in competing for this business.

These examples highlight why hidden assets are so important to the economics of serving next-generation demand. They also offer huge investment leverage advantages. Once a hidden asset is created, it can usually be extended or reused at little or no cost. This means that the marginal economics of such hidden assets as a great brand name, a strategic position in the value chain, or the power of a unique software application are extremely attractive. If used skillfully in building next-generation offerings, they can help lower the cost of customer acquisition, reduce the cost of development, and accelerate the ramp-up of the business. The result is a significantly enhanced return on the original investment in the asset and better, faster returns from the new business.

By contrast, expanding the use of a traditional tangible asset is usually expensive. For example, increasing the output of a factory may require enlarging the plant, buying more machinery, and hiring additional workers.

Hidden assets differ from physical assets in another crucial way: When leveraged, they tend to multiply. The more you use them, the more you have. Relationships become stronger. Information becomes richer and deeper. Networks become more extended. And so on.

Hidden assets can also help create powerful competitive barriers because they are difficult and expensive to replicate. In today's economy, a company can outsource engineering, manufacturing, distribution, even selling, and build a virtual competitor overnight. Handspring did this in the palm computing market and went on to grab a leading share. But hidden assets such as IBM's customer relationships, Coca-Cola's brand, and Schwab's market position all took decades of work and billions of dollars to create. As a result, they represent powerful and unique sources of differentiation that an upstart couldn't hope to match without spending a prohibitive amount of time and money.

Types of Hidden Assets

There's a wide array of hidden assets, many of which are rarely thought of as assets at all. We've identified eighteen primary hidden assets in five major categories. Depending on the nature of your business, each may be a potential source of sustainable future growth.

In the pages that follow, we'll describe each of the five categories. As you read, ask yourself:

- Which of these hidden assets does your company own?
- What kind of hidden assets *not* listed here does your company own?
- How might your hidden assets be relevant to addressing new customer demand?

Traditional Intangible Assets

These are hidden assets with which most managers are already familiar. They include *intellectual property and content* (like the movies, images, and characters owned by Disney or the patents owned by Intel), *methods and core competencies* (the unique manufacturing capabilities of Toyota), and *brands* (those owned by Virgin, McDonald's, and Coca-Cola).

Customer Relationships

A company's customer relationships can be a critical gateway to addressing unmet customer needs. Having a powerful set of customer relationships is a little like being the oldest, best-known, and most respected merchant in town—Marshall Field in Chicago or Filene's in Boston.

Customer relationship assets take a variety of forms. They can significantly cut the time and expense of customer acquisition relative to new entrants, generate more sophisticated customer offerings developed more precisely and at lower cost, and improve the acceptance rate and premium pricing of new services. For example, John Deere leveraged its *customer authority* in the green market—its presumed expertise and credibility in agriculture and lawn care—in launching John Deere Landscapes.

Wal-Mart and Coca-Cola have great *reach*. They touch lots of customers and can therefore bring scale marketing to any new idea.

Others have a unique level of *customer interaction*. For example, Hanover Compressor, a leading producer of natural gas compressors for oil and gas recovery, is driven by the need to frequently observe and reassess compressor needs as wells mature. This interaction gives Hanover an up-to-the-minute understanding of customer needs, which it has used to expand its business into a host of new areas.

Some companies like Capital One have developed deep *insight* into their customers' economic issues and challenges, which allows them to anticipate rather than respond to customer needs. Capital One's unique system for microanalyzing consumer credit needs and risks enables it not only to offer credit to thousands of customers whom other companies deem ineligible, but also to transform seemingly unpromising market segments into highly profitable ones.

Strategic Real Estate

Strategic real estate assets are defined by where a company sits in its industry. Owning a valuable piece of strategic real estate is comparable to owning the most desirable corner location on New York's Fifth Avenue or Los Angeles's Rodeo Drive; it can create significant speed and cost advantages in entering new markets relative to upstarts or less well-positioned competitors.

DeWolfe Homeowner Services originated as a real estate brokerage company. This brokerage role provided an ideal *market position* from which to enter related markets such as mortgage and insurance brokering, since DeWolfe owned the first transaction in the home-buying process that triggers the need for these other services.

Another form of strategic real estate is an advantaged position in the industry *value chain* that provides preferential access to new growth opportunities. As a drug distributor, Cardinal was uniquely positioned to offer new services both downstream to hospitals and drugstores and upstream to drug producers.

Still another kind of strategic real estate asset is ownership of the *portal or access point* to information or services. This can be offline, as with Schwab's mutual fund supermarket, or online, as with the cable companies' digital set-top boxes.

Enterprise Networks

Enterprise network assets are based on a company's extended view of the business and its key constituents, which can provide a unique opportunity to offer customers new products and services. Having a powerful set of network assets is like being the Hollywood agent with the best Rolodex in town—one that lists not only Steven Spielberg's office and home, but also his ultraprivate cell phone number.

General Motors has built OnStar into the leading mobile services company by leveraging one important type of network asset, its access to the large *installed base* of GM vehicles that dramatically lowered its customer acquisition costs. Another network asset is *third-party relationships* with suppliers, channels, and universities. IBM has taken advantage of its reselling relationship with many software vendors to develop its large Global Services consulting and systems integration business.

A company's *user community* is the group of customers who see value in interacting among themselves to share issues, information, and experiences. Harley-Davidson has used its famously large and loyal Harley Owners Group to create a mystique around its product and to spur significant sales of motorcycle-related lifestyle and after-market products.

Deal flow is yet another type of network asset. In some industries, one company has privileged access to all the best new business ideas and technologies because of its locations at the center of a strategic network. In the chain restaurant business, McDonald's has that role; in networking gear, it's Cisco Systems.

Information

Information assets are the most overlooked and underutilized hidden assets. Although companies have made huge investments in software, systems, and networks to capture and manipulate information about their businesses over the past decade, few companies have used their investments as a springboard for serving customers' new needs and for creating next-generation growth.

Specific information assets include *systems and software* that can be repurposed from internal needs to serving customers. A good example is the Sabre reservations system business that American Airlines built for the travel industry, using its proprietary schedule planning and tracking software.

Technical know-how can be a valuable hidden asset, as demonstrated by the profits such companies as Air Liquide, DuPont, and Bosch have generated by applying their technical knowledge to addressing new customer needs.

Shell and Cargill have built businesses based on the *market window* they own. In each case, information flows through the company because of the many market transactions it participates in as a middleman or supplier. This information about the ebbs and flows of supply and demand provides valuable market intelligence that can fuel market making, brokering, and trading activities.

A fourth type of information asset is *by-product information*. Cardinal's ArcLight business, built around the packaging and selling of existing retail pharmacy sales information to pharmaceutical manufacturers, is a good example.

Necessary but Not Sufficient: Building Your Asset System

Hidden assets are critical components in the process of turning demand innovation into profits, but they can't do the job alone. Think of hidden assets as a crucial element of a comprehensive *asset system* that includes all the assets required to deliver on a business promise. This asset system also includes the important tangible assets needed to make the business work, the capabilities one needs to acquire, and the additional assets that are built along the way.

For instance, when Johnson Controls shifted its focus to delivering seating and interior systems, its market position gave it a vital and differentiated entry point. But this advantage had to be augmented with the development of new engineering and testing skills, the acquisition of broader manufacturing capabilities, and a new focus on senior-level selling.

Both acquired and internally built assets are important to keeping the new business vibrant and on a continued path of differentiation and evolution. Just as a focus on meeting next-generation demand often uncovers additional needs that can be served, a focus on building a powerful asset system often leads to the creation of new hidden assets that can be leveraged in exciting ways.

Mastering the New Discipline of Demand Innovation

Learning to mobilize your hidden assets in support of demand innovation requires a significant mental adjustment, a rethinking of habits you've probably spent years developing. The shift from traditional growth to demand innovation operates along many dimensions:

- From viewing your business through a product lens to studying your customers through an economic lens.
- From creating growth based on traditional tools (products, factories, personnel) to creating growth based on hidden assets (relationships, market position, information).
- From thinking of company size as a growth

inhibitor to thinking of size as a multiplier of growth opportunities.

- From worrying that marginal growth will cannibalize your base business to building new-growth initiatives that reinforce and strengthen your base.
- From relying on blockbuster new products to revolutionize your market to developing a trajectory of evolutionary, customer-centric moves based on structured creativity and operating discipline.
- From scrambling to eke out margin points in a world of diminishing opportunity to expanding your horizons to include an arena five to ten times larger than your traditional market space.
- From being a product supplier to being an economic partner.
- From being a demand taker to being a demand innovator.

Managers who master these critical new ways of thinking will be able to generate meaningful long-term growth. For those who don't, the growth crisis will continue to worsen.

Finally, one caveat. Not every business in every industry is in a position to identify and serve next-generation demand. Some may occupy market niches so narrowly defined and so hemmed in by competitors that they have no choice but to accept a low-growth or no-growth future. Such companies may be able to survive in the financial markets as low-risk, low-reward holdings that attract investors who seek income, not growth. This is an honorable role to fill, if not an exciting one. However, before relegating your company to this fate, we urge you to read part 2. The companies whose stories are told in these five chapters have created innovative and highly profitable next-generation growth in very daunting environments.

Reading about how these companies succeeded in the quest for growth will help you learn a different way of thinking. You will gain a deeper sense of what it means to think in terms of shaping new demand and the unique hidden assets that will help you create breakout, high-intensity growth. You may even see elements of your company's growth situation and market dynamics mirrored in these stories, which can help you frame approaches to solving your own growth crisis.

PART TWO

The Demand Innovators

5

"The Large-Number Issue Is Huge for Us": GM OnStar

General Motors faces a challenge peculiar to very large companies: It has an enormous base business that dwarfs almost all new-growth initiatives, making any such move seem trivial. Yet GM has found a way to make new growth pay by looking for opportunities to create businesses that are capable of driving profit growth at a rate disproportionate to their modest size. OnStar, a unique offering of safety and security services enabled by special in-vehicle electronics, is viewed by GM as just such a high-intensity business. But what does GM, a quintessential manufacturing company, bring to the high-tech arena of vehicle communications services?

Too Big to Grow?

When it comes to pursuing next-generation growth opportunities, General Motors, the world's largest automaker, wrestles with an acute "large-number problem." GM's automobile manufacturing business generated revenue of $141 billion in 2001. The idea of launching a new-growth initiative that will expand that figure by an appreciable percentage is daunting. There aren't many new business ideas that will quickly generate $10 billion or more. Thus, as CEO Rick Wagoner puts it, "The large-number issue is huge for us. It is simply not possible to grow this business at 5 to 8 percent a year *without* growing the core."

Recognizing this reality, GM has developed a growth program that is largely focused on enhancing its base business. Key elements of the plan include a renewed emphasis on vehicle styling and engineering, the development of profitable niche models (particularly in the highly lucrative truck market where GM excels), more focus on high-margin add-ons and accessories, and more astute merchandising, advertising, and incentive programs to drive dealer traffic and sales volume. The approach is paying off. During 2001, GM gained market share and left the rest of the industry scrambling to match its moves.

But GM's management team also recognizes that improving the base auto business alone will not be enough. Even Toyota, considered by many to be the most successful auto company in the world, has just a 7.6 percent operating margin, a 3 percent return on assets, and low-single-digit annual sales growth. Most other auto companies have numbers that look a lot worse. GM's management and stakeholders want to do better.

The solution developed by Wagoner and his team is to continue to push hard at growing the base business, but also look for opportunities to supplement that growth with a few high-intensity profit drivers in peripheral but related businesses. Think of them as cars with souped-up, high-performance engines capable of delivering bottom-line growth out of proportion to their size.

One such business is GMAC, the financing arm of GM. Originally created in the 1920s to provide installment financing for cars, GMAC has gradually expanded its activities to include full-service leasing and extended service contracts. Most recently, GMAC has built a very successful home mortgage business that leverages GM's access to funds and securitization skills as well as its reputation as a solid consumer finance company.

GM's management is looking for similar opportunities, new but related engines of profit that can contribute more than their share to the corporation's bottom line. In the mid-1990s, it looked as if they might have discovered one. It was a business concept that used new technologies in an exciting way to address many of the latent issues associated with owning and driving a car.

Me and My Car

No consumer product transcends the category of mere product more dramatically than the automobile. People invest huge amounts of time, energy, money, and emotion in their cars. A new car is the second most expensive thing most people ever buy after a house. Some of our most joyful and liberating experiences are associated with cars: a cross-country trek, a summer drive with the top down and the stereo wailing, or parking by a moonlit beach. But so are some of our most frustrating, unnerving, and dangerous experiences: negotiating a rain- or snow-slick highway, sitting for hours stuck in traffic, getting lost on poorly marked roads, or dealing with an accident.

It's not surprising, then, that a whole industry has grown up to serve the needs associated with owning an automobile. In the U.S., car dealers, insurers, the American Automobile Association, and local mechanics are all part of a trillion-dollar industry dedicated to keeping drivers happily on the road. Unfortunately, this support network often falls short of expectations. It is fragmented among disparate providers, it is often unavailable when or where it is needed, and it neglects the softer needs associated with traveling by car, such as feeling safe and in control, making productive use of time on the road, and getting help in deciding where to go and how to get there.

Today, as leisure time feels more scarce and the

daily commute grows longer, we spend more and more time in our cars—nearly eight hours a week, according to one study—making these softer needs more acute. Surely there's a business—or several businesses—to be built around this powerful collection of desires, emotions, and needs that surround our cars.

Electronic Horizons

In the mid-1990s, engineers within several GM business units realized that technological advances might enable the creation of a new business focused on the softer needs of drivers. Thanks to breakthroughs in digital mapping, satellite navigation, and mobile communications, drivers might be able to access a collection of information, support, and even entertainment services like those the telephone, the personal computer, and the cell phone had already brought to the home and the office.

At first blush, the potential value of such communications services in the car might seem modest. But 65 percent of all cell phone calls are made from cars, and millions of drivers have better stereo systems in their automobiles than they do in their homes. The growing number of hours spent in the car only increases drivers' need for information, diversion, and relaxation. It was clear that the opportunity here was real, large, and growing.

Motivated by this vision, GM engineers developed

a new mobile hardware system and service package they called OnStar. The hardware includes a cellular phone, a global positioning system (GPS) receiver, two antennas, a three-button control panel, and a modem. The services fall into two broad categories. The first group focuses on safety and security issues. In an emergency, for example, a driver need only touch the red OnStar button on the dashboard. This alerts a call center adviser, who locates the vehicle via GPS and contacts the nearest 911 service to send help. The same thing happens automatically whenever a vehicle's airbag deploys. Other security features include remote door unlocking, theft tracking, and vehicle warning light diagnostics.

A second group of services offers ways of making car travel more convenient and fun. An OnStar adviser can provide directions to any destination or help drivers find the nearest gas station, rest stop, or repair shop. In fact, OnStar has built a database with five million entries listing bank branches, movie theaters, restaurants, hotels, shopping malls, campsites, and other locations nationwide.

Acting as concierge, an OnStar adviser can also help drivers with a range of personal services including vacation planning, ticket purchases for plays, concerts, and sporting events, hotel reservations, and so on. Drivers can call OnStar from the road, ask for directions to the nearest Chinese restaurant, and have the adviser book a corner table.

In 1995, with its technology in place, OnStar was launched as a freestanding business unit within GM's North American Operations. Chet Huber, the forty-year-old executive chosen to lead the new venture, brought a couple of unusual qualities to the assignment. He was a respected insider with a long GM tenure and strong senior management relationships, but also somewhat of an outsider. He came not from the Detroit auto business but from GM's Illinois-based Electromotive division. At Electromotive, he'd had the rare experience for a GM manager of running his own P&L relatively early in his career. Huber's inside/outside perspective and his experience managing a self-contained business would prove important in launching OnStar.

A New Kind of Business

At first, OnStar was viewed by many GM executives as the newest embodiment of a long tradition of adding features such as moon roofs to cars. Its value would be as an exclusive amenity that would help promote new-vehicle sales.

As Chet Huber and his leadership team worked to commercialize OnStar, however, they began to evolve a new perspective on the nature of the OnStar business. As a mobile information service, OnStar would have economic characteristics very different from those of the traditional auto business—or from any mere auto feature or accessory.

Rather than simply helping enable a vehicle purchase (a onetime transaction), OnStar could launch a recurring stream of monthly subscription revenues, conceivably for the life of the vehicle. The target market for this subscription business was actually significantly broader than the market of five million new vehicles that GM sells every year. Instead, over time it would encompass all eighty million GM vehicles on the road. A successful OnStar had a shot at owning a recurring revenue stream from a decent share of this large market.

Thus, OnStar could be in a different category from traditional automotive amenities. If launched and developed effectively, it could represent a new form of value capture for GM and a significant revenue growth opportunity in its own right—provided that the new service could be quickly made available to a large number of drivers.

Stalled Engine

This vision of OnStar was an enticing one. But it would not be easy to achieve the widespread availability and acceptance necessary to turn it into reality.

The initial distribution strategy for OnStar quickly emerged as a major stumbling block. At launch, OnStar was designated for dealer installation on just one model, the 1997 Cadillac DeVille. As with other add-on amenities like DVD players and rear spoilers, this meant that the Cadillac dealer would be responsible for selling, installing, and briefing the customer about OnStar.

Unfortunately, the cost and price realities of On-

Star created challenges for the dealers. Most dealer-installed accessories are sold at a significant markup. By contrast, the recommended hardware price of $895 for OnStar included a dealer margin of just 20 percent. This made OnStar a relatively unattractive proposition for most dealers. The economics of the distribution channel weren't so good for OnStar either. At the $895 price, OnStar was subsidizing a significant portion of the total hardware cost.

A second distribution challenge was educating and training the Cadillac dealers to sell OnStar effectively. There are fifteen hundred Cadillac dealers across the United States. In order for them to successfully sell OnStar to their customers, each dealer had to be trained by GM to understand the true value and appeal of OnStar—a time-consuming and complicated task, especially given the innovative nature of the service.

Not surprisingly, OnStar fell short of its initial sales targets. By the end of 1998, OnStar had only forty-four thousand paying subscribers rather than the hundred thousand GM had hoped for.

By all accounts, however, drivers who used OnStar liked the service. OnStar enhanced its customers' experience with their cars and was successfully addressing such next-generation needs as safety, security, and freedom.

Consider the case of Susan Frank. Driving home to Mississippi from a family vacation in Florida with a full load of passengers in her Cadillac Seville, Frank was hit by another car trying to pass her on a wet roadway. OnStar immediately notified local police and rescue units, and an OnStar adviser contacted Frank's husband to alert him.

Reflecting on the experience later, Susan Frank commented, "I cannot tell you how thankful I am to be alive today with my family intact. My Seville was totaled. I am driving a new Escalade, with OnStar of course. I would not be without it. It was a lifesaver for four women and three small children who were 160 miles from home."

Such stories testified to OnStar's value. Yet GM had yet to figure out how to make the business into the high-intensity profit driver they were seeking. The first half of the new-growth equation was in place: Customers liked the service immensely. The second half of the equation, signing up a large number of customers, still had to be resolved.

This was a major challenge. The service was slated for a relatively measured rollout onto other GM vehicles, adding just a handful of other Cadillac models to its lineup over the next few years. Moving faster would be difficult. OnStar can't be dropped easily into a new vehicle, but must be connected to many of the car's electronic components, from airbags to diagnostic sensors to door locks and headlights. Getting OnStar to work correctly requires a complicated design and testing process known as *validation*, which takes up to six months per vehicle model to complete. In addition, given the big hardware subsidy it was laying out on each unit, GM had mixed emotions about ramping up OnStar's availability.

Meanwhile, potential competitors were beginning to emerge. They included carmakers such as Ford, with its RESCU offering; start-ups like ATX Technologies, which offered a luxury communications system to owners of BMW, Mercedes-Benz, Lincoln, and Jaguar vehicles; and the juggernaut Microsoft, which was signaling its intention to build an "auto PC." In combination, these competitors might steal the market out from under GM or, even worse, turn mobile services into simply another expected auto feature, like airbags or power windows.

So here was OnStar, technically impressive, lauded by customers—but expensive to deploy, narrowly available, dependent on dealers for distribution, and with a burgeoning list of all-too-similar aftermarket competitors nipping at its heels.

To survive and win, OnStar had to grow—and fast.

At a Crossroads

Huber's leadership team, together with the top leadership at GM, considered several moves to jump-start OnStar's growth.

One possibility was to focus on improving the training, marketing support, and financial incentives provided to dealers. This would be the simplest, least costly, and least risky choice. But at best, it promised only incremental improvement in sales and little advantage in building this business.

A more challenging path called for shifting from dealer installation of the hardware to factory installation. This would eliminate a lot of the dealers' issues. More important, factory installation would allow GM to leverage its one significant advantage in building a mobile services business: its unique access to the huge *installed base* of GM-produced vehicles.

GM sells five million vehicles in North America annually, more than any other manufacturer, and it controls exactly what goes on each of those vehicles as they pass through the assembly plant. By installing OnStar directly in the factory, GM could gain significant advantages versus its competitors in building out a mobile services subscriber base.

The first of these advantages is customer access. By making OnStar part of a popular factory-installed option package, GM would be able to bypass the vagaries of the dealer-selling process. Factory installation could also significantly lower the cost to acquire and provision an OnStar customer. It would eliminate the need to provide dealer commissions and cut out expensive dealer-installation charges. Best of all, the simplicity of factory installation would significantly reduce the cost of the hardware itself. Overall, factory installation would give GM close to a 70 percent cost improvement in acquiring a new customer, making it profitable to OnStar much more quickly. Any competitor without the ability to offer factory-installation would be at an extreme cost disadvantage.

It could also—potentially—allow GM to introduce OnStar on a wider array of car models more quickly than previously planned, creating important long-term advantages.

Chet Huber and his team understood that market

penetration would play a big role in determining On-Star's long-term profitability. Having more customers would drive down equipment costs, call centers and supporting information systems could be amortized across a broader base of users, and third-party service and technology providers would likely come calling OnStar first.

This last insight suggested a third option that was even bolder: to broaden the potential market for On-Star by making it available on non-GM car models.

Recruiting other original equipment manufacturers (OEMs) to share OnStar offered some huge potential benefits. Most significantly, if GM moved quickly enough (and enjoyed a little good luck along the way), OnStar might become the de facto standard of the nascent in-vehicle services industry.

The advantages of building a de facto standard business design in any technology are significant. The leading technology in any field attracts an increasing share of subsidiary technologies from software developers and content suppliers. It gains the cost benefits that come with scale, making the economics of mounting a competitive challenge harder for potential competitors. It also produces snow-balling network effects, as the data flow from a huge mass of existing customers makes it possible to develop still more valuable information and service offerings.

With the entire mobile services business in its infancy, OnStar was as well positioned as any company to establish the de facto standard. But pursuing this goal would require breaking with the traditional car industry culture. It would mean pushing GM's core automotive business to bend its vehicle development cycles to accelerate the validation process. It would also mean "giving" competing firms a proprietary technology that GM had spent millions of dollars to develop.

Most important, it would mean changing the relationship between the parent company and its off-spring. OnStar would have to become a connected-yet-independent business free to work with automakers other than GM in markets around the world, to build its own customer base, and to de-velop and promote its own brand name.

Breakout

In early 1999, GM's leadership made two tough choices. One was to make OnStar a factory-installed option on a wide array of new GM vehicles, not just on Cadillacs. The other was to pursue the goal of making OnStar the de facto standard of the new in-vehicle services business, available through multiple carmakers.

In combination, these moves produced a dramatic growth explosion for OnStar. The Cadillac Escalade, a luxury sport utility vehicle, was the first GM model to get OnStar as a factory-installed option. The pos-itive effects were large and immediate. By mid-1999, 42 percent of Escalade buyers called OnStar a factor in their decision to buy a Cadillac. OnStar was beginning not only to attract revenues in its own right but also to benefit GM's core business.

OnStar engineering teams pushed hard to accelerate the validation process for more GM models. To help speed this process, the former vehicle line engineer for the Cadillac Catera was hired to run a new group in charge of hardware systems development. The job involved managing an ongoing series of mini crises and coping with the pressure of meeting production schedules so as not to delay the release of a new car model. GM's senior managers also played a key role in accelerating OnStar's validation and rollout schedule. They intervened with the powerful vehicle engineers to make OnStar validation a priority. This not only helped speed things up, but also signaled that GM was serious enough about OnStar to tinker with the sacrosanct vehicle development process.

With each successful launch of a new OnStar vehicle platform, the process became a little easier and faster. By mid-2002, OnStar was available on thirty-eight of GM's fifty-two models.

OnStar also used another important hidden asset, its web of industry relationships and alliances, to reach out to other carmakers. Most notably, chairman Jack Smith opened the first door by calling his friend Hiroshi Okuda, chairman of Toyota, whom he'd met earlier in his career when the two had collaborated in building the innovative GM-Toyota NUMMI production facility.

Today, OnStar is available on cars made by Lexus (Toyota's luxury brand), Audi, Acura, Isuzu, Saab, and Subaru, with more automakers coming online every year. Broad acceptance of the OnStar brand has been critical to building OnStar into the leading in-vehicle services provider both within the industry and among consumers.

On the consumer side, OnStar's brand building was boosted by the success of a television ad campaign featuring Batman using OnStar in the Batmobile as a tool in his crime-fighting adventures. OnStar has invested more than $100 million in brand support since the campaign's launch in January 2000, and consumer awareness has soared.

Coping with Growth

By early 2002, more than two million vehicles were equipped with OnStar, as compared to fewer than fifty thousand three years earlier. This figure is forecast to grow to over four million by the end of 2003.

As a result, OnStar is now coping with the challenges of rapid growth. The company has absorbed hundreds of new employees, most from outside the car business, with all the managerial and human challenges that implies. Giant call centers in Michigan and North Carolina have been staffed with hundreds of college-educated advisers who must survive a tough six-week training program. Every month, the advisers find 375 stolen cars, respond to three hundred airbag deployments, and unlock fifteen thousand sets of car doors. And the numbers keep growing.

To keep up with the challenges, GM has worked hard to bring in talent in important new functions like key account sales, often from related industries such as computers and telecom. In fact, two-thirds of all OnStar employees come from outside GM. OnStar has also focused on creating outside alliances to access markets, develop new services, and evolve its technology. To support this pollination, OnStar set up its advanced development operations in Silicon Valley—tapping new ideas and new talent pools in the process.

Winning Phase One

OnStar today serves 80 percent of all U.S. mobile services customers. Potential competitors for OnStar are lagging as Ford's RESCU has fizzled and ATX's luxury offering is profitable but remains a niche business.

Despite the newness of the mobile services business, OnStar's status as industry leader is already producing competitive benefits. Having OnStar up and running in two million vehicles gives the company both a depth and breadth of technical expertise would-be competitors will be hard-pressed to match, as well as a big advantage in cost-to-serve economics.

Consider, for example, the complexity of connecting OnStar's call centers with other links in the service network, such as the hundreds of local 911 centers. When you buy a home security system, the monitoring service sets up a simple link to the local police and fire departments—your house isn't going anywhere. But your car can crash around the corner or across the country. That means OnStar had to solve the complex task of ensuring instant access to local 911 centers everywhere. That's a tough move for a competitor to follow and pay for.

Challenges to Come

GM's vision for OnStar doesn't stop with its first-generation safety and security and diagnostic services. A key element of the company's growth strategy is to build out from a new business platform once it begins to show promise rather than scattering investments across lots of subscale, disconnected efforts. OnStar is rapidly evolving into just such a platform.

To be sure, OnStar is moving carefully with service expansion. Chet Huber's philosophy on this is clear: OnStar will focus on getting all the basics right before rushing out new services. Huber reasons that if early adapters are disappointed with OnStar, bad word of mouth will damage the brand and slow the development of the business.

OnStar has launched several new services since 2001. One is Personal Calling, a hands-free mobile phone service in partnership with Verizon. This opens the door to a new profit stream for OnStar via the buying and reselling of cell phone minutes—in fact, OnStar is already the largest cellular service reseller in the country. Another is Virtual Advisor, a customized, voice-activated information service that provides drivers with traffic and weather reports, sports scores, stock quotes, and even delivery of e-mail messages read aloud by an automated voice. It's a prototype of the information and entertainment services that could end up as commonplace parts of the mobile services bundle.

GM is starting to build additional services into OnStar, ranging from mobile transactions and in-vehicle entertainment to dynamic traffic and route assistance. GM has invested in XM Radio, a satellite radio system offering a hundred digital channels of music, news, and chat for a monthly subscription fee of $9.95. XM Radio is available exclusively on GM new vehicles as a factory-installed option, and GM will garner royalties on all XM subscriptions sold to GM drivers. Once again, OnStar is leveraging GM's massive installed base to lower deployment costs and spur consumer adoption. So far, XM Radio is one of the fastest-growing new consumer services ever, with more than 135,000 subscribers signed up since the launch of nationwide service in November 2001.

Future OnStar offerings are already being explored. Most information and entertainment currently available via radio, television, and the Internet could be adapted for the car, and many would undoubtedly find an audience. Each subgroup of drivers will probably regard a different service as the "killer app" that motivates them to buy and keep OnStar.

As the number of OnStar vehicles on the road increases, so do the opportunities for network effects. For example, unique traffic data available only to OnStar customers could be compiled by monitoring the location and speed of OnStar-equipped vehicles. If cars traveling north on the Sprain Brook Parkway are moving faster than cars on the parallel Bronx River Parkway, OnStar could alert subscribers to save time by switching highways.

OnStar could also support the nascent business of selling metered car insurance, in which rates are based on where, how, and how much you drive. Progressive Insurance is already experimenting with this approach, but OnStar could help make the necessary metering extremely accurate and efficient.

Measuring OnStar's Success

The development of new communications technologies made mobile services feasible by the mid-1990s. Any of the world's big automakers might have created the equivalent of OnStar. So could a range of high-tech outfits, from PC makers to software firms to consumer electronics companies. Yet so far, only GM has fully developed the opportunity. What has made the difference? The crucial factors in GM's success have been its ability to look at customers' driving needs from a fresh perspective (one very different from a traditional carmaker's focus on performance, fuel efficiency, and features) and its decision to serve these needs through a business design that leverages GM's unique hidden asset—its unequaled installed base of vehicles.

While OnStar is just now maturing as a business model, it is on its way to becoming one of those high-impact growth opportunities that GM has sought. OnStar is approaching $1 billion in annual revenue. This may look tiny next to GM's $180 billion in total revenue, but OnStar provides revenue with high-contribution margin. Once the initial hardware installation has been paid off, subscription fees drop almost entirely to the bottom line. As OnStar focuses on enhancing customer retention rates and driving up monthly fees through new services, its performance should only improve.

This is not unlike the characteristics of other installed-base businesses, such as CNN, *USA Today,* and the Discover Card. For each of these businesses, reaching breakeven took five to seven years of investment, but significant profits followed.

Has all of this effort, new thinking by GM managers and Chet Huber and his team, and exhaustive attention to the details behind the service been worth it? CEO Rick Wagoner puts it this way: "OnStar represents an important part of our strategy of having a number of these high-intensity profit drivers in our portfolio—businesses that are smaller today but have the potential to create outsized returns. For us, they represent the critical difference between a solid company and one with momentum and expanding prospects for growth in the stock price."

Taking a Page from OnStar's Playbook

If you work in a traditional product-centered manufacturing firm, there may be a significant growth opportunity in the areas surrounding your product's installed base. Here are some relevant questions:

- GM found new, unmet needs in an otherwise mature industry by expanding its view of the market. Can you identify one or more adjacent market spaces with high-intensity growth and profit potential?
- OnStar sought to address the emotional and empowerment issues associated with improving the car driving experience. Do your customers have "soft" emotional needs that might be addressed in innovative ways?
- GM's installed base represents an asset that would be virtually impossible for a new competitor to replicate. Does your core business generate any assets that are similarly difficult to match?

6

"If You're Not Talking to the Customer, Someone Else Is": Clarke American

Clarke American, the third largest provider of checks to financial institutions in the United States, has been able to grow its business substantially by transforming itself into a provider of customer management solutions for its financial institution partners. How was Clarke American able to effect such a radical change? And why are financial institutions letting a mere check printer take on such an important role?

A Gathering Storm

Fifteen years ago, check printing was a tidy little business protected by high barriers to entry. In the old days of hot-metal letterpress, printing was done on intricate, oily machines that cost a lot of money to maintain and took a lot of know-how to operate. Printing checks was especially complicated. The job included two stages, first printing the safety paper background and then personalizing the check itself. It involved working with difficult magnetic inks and secure databases of consumer account information. And it required running many small lots of customized documents quickly and with near-perfect accuracy.

Throw in the cultural conservatism of the customer base—banks and credit unions—and the fact that neither consumers nor banks focused on the cost of a check, and you have a stable industry with little competitive pressure and relatively high profit margins.

In that tidy world, Clarke American had built itself into one of the biggest and most profitable players. After a series of acquisitions, it was the third largest check printer and it was known for its product and service quality.

But this comfortable situation would prove to be vulnerable as several trends converged to create problems in the 1990s.

Beginning in the mid-1980s, the financial services business had been undergoing consolidation, creating a bifurcated industry. The community banks and credit unions no longer predominated. Meanwhile, the larger institutions were growing much larger, as local banks acquired one another and were transformed first into state banks, then into regional banks, and in many cases into national banks. These large entities established central purchasing units to handle outsourced functions such as check printing. As the check product offering matured, purchasing managers increasingly focused on price, and the reliably high profit margins of check providers began to come under pressure.

At the same time, the number of checks written by bank customers stopped growing and eventually started to decline, thanks to the advent of online banking and the increased popularity of pay-by-phone, credit cards, and debit cards. In this tough environment, Clarke American had to work hard to reduce costs and take out waste to keep its profits from shrinking.

But that wasn't all. Other trends on the supply side began squeezing Clarke American. Printing underwent a major technological change from traditional letterpress to offset, which drastically reduced the cost and complexity of printing equipment and hence the value of the big printing plants owned by Clarke American and the other incumbents. And there was the emergence of a new competitive force, the direct suppliers who sold checks cheaply to consumers via direct mail advertising and fliers in newspapers and later the Internet. Coming from nowhere, these upstarts grew to claim 20 percent of the market by the end of the decade.

As these trends converged, the check printing business was pushed toward commoditization, and Clarke American could see a major revenue and earnings crisis on the horizon. The company's first response, like that of its competitors, was to cut costs and consolidate plants, but that was enough only to stem the decline, not to reverse it.

By the mid-1990s, these trends were taking their toll. Chuck Dawson, senior vice president and general manager of national accounts at Clarke American, recalls what happened as several big contracts came up for renegotiation at this time: "Pricing was a big part of the decision criteria, and the resulting terms dramatically affected our operating margin. It was clear we had a crisis on our hands. We knew we had to do something about it. But we didn't know what."

Avoiding the Core Competency Trap

In response to the profit crisis, Clarke American's executive team, led by its new CEO Charles Korbell, used their focus on Total Quality Management, with its emphasis on long-range strategic planing, to undertake a review of the growth options available to them.

Should they go into related printing businesses? After all, Clarke American was a specialized, high-quality custom printer with unique technical expertise in short-run printing. Maybe this core competency could be applied to other products and other markets. Clarke American could begin producing stamps, labels, business forms, and stationery. It could get into longer-run check printing for insurance companies or government agencies.

On close examination, however, these opportunities proved less than exciting. For one thing, all of these businesses were already populated by successful competitors that knew the markets better than Clarke American did. For another, the same trends that were knocking down entry barriers and pricing supports in check printing were at work in these markets. Why expand from one commoditizing business into a series of other businesses that were commoditizing just as quickly?

Clarke American's leadership realized that its traditional core competency, customized specialty printing, was no longer a strong enough platform on which to build new growth businesses. Clarke American had learned an important lesson: Clinging to a core competency and attempting to ride it into new markets may seem like a natural thing to do in times of a growth crisis. But often your company's competencies are no more valuable in those new markets.

A New Take on the Marketplace

Korbell and his team realized that to reverse the decline in profits and grow their share in a flat to declining market, they needed a new approach to their banking partners. (Clarke American refers to its financial institution customers as *partners*, reserving the word *customers* for the ultimate users of banking services—its customers' customers.)

The new approach began with a recognition of

how the financial services industry was changing. If financial institutions were being divided into two segments—a few giants and thousands of others—then it made sense to reorganize the company to provide value to these very different categories of customers. To do so, Clarke American would embark on a new, multistep strategy to target each segment of its bank and credit union partners for special attention and then develop new capabilities and services to meet their most pressing needs.

To make this concept a reality, the company initiated a strategic account program in 1994 that was built around four critical elements:

- *Screen current and potential partners* to select the best opportunities on which to concentrate. This included assessing not only Clarke American's revenue and profit potential but also softer issues such as whether the financial institutions were at the leading edge or lagging in terms of customer focus, and whether they were likely to be buyers or sellers in the continuing industry consolidation.
- *Reorganize the Clarke American sales force* from its traditional geographic structure in which a salesperson called on every bank or branch in a region to a customer-segment-oriented structure where salespeople were dedicated to large key accounts, community banks, or credit unions.
- *Create new partner relationships* that were broader and deeper and included senior managers and the executives responsible for consumer marketing, not just purchasing. If needed, Clarke American

would build or hire the new skills needed to create such relationships with the ultimate goal of becoming part of the financial institution's strategic planning process.

- *Change sales force incentives* from rewarding the winning of new business—no matter how small or unprofitable—to rewarding relationship maintenance, customer satisfaction, and the growth of existing accounts.

This change in the selling model was an important shift. It meant that Clarke American was now focusing on actively identifying strategic opportunities to help its bank clients grow profitability and investing in these opportunities. It also meant a shift away from pursuing sales growth for its own sake. As Charles Korbell says, "Our emphasis shifted to finding ways to help our partners improve the experience of their customers. The message to potential partners became, if you understand and share this vision, and would like to work with us, we'll make it more profitable for everybody."

Keeping Customers and Keeping Them Happy

Identifying partners with the greatest future potential and interest in better serving their customers was the first part of the new growth strategy. The second part was uncovering new ways for Clarke American to serve these partners.

The high-level conversations now taking place between Clarke American and its strategic partners quickly made clear that the most important next-generation need that its partners faced was to retain customers and deepen relationships in an increasingly competitive climate. This insight led directly to a strategic opportunity for Clarke American: the need for conversion support.

Conversion refers to all the tasks required to maintain customer service when one bank acquires another. It includes integrating account databases, combining check ordering processes, handling customer inquiries, and getting newly printed checks out to the acquired customers.

Smooth conversions were extremely important to acquiring banks, which were under tremendous pressure from investors to demonstrate that they could handle serial bank acquisitions without jeopardizing customer relationships. Poorly handled mergers weren't just a cost or customer service issue. They could lop millions of dollars from a bank's market value.

Clarke American stepped up to this opportunity by creating a comprehensive conversion management program to handle all the checking account conversion tasks for the bank, including communications with the end customer about the changeover.

What hidden assets did Clarke American use to make this program work? The answer is an array of skills and capabilities drawn from the company's base business, including its long-standing reputation for accuracy and timeliness in check printing, and the ability to update and integrate databases. These assets meant that Clarke American could deliver conversion services more efficiently and cost-effectively than anyone else.

The strategic partner program was the icing on the cake. It gave Clarke American relationships with the financial institution managers needed to approve such a role and conveyed the company's seriousness about demonstrating the value of partnership.

Clarke American earned new fees from its conversion services. It also nicely shifted the relationship from one built around simple check printing services and centered on the purchasing department to a collaboration around merger effectiveness involving the bank's senior managers. The bank, in turn, protected its shareholder value and its relationships with the end customers, which were so critical to its own future growth.

Perhaps most important, the move into conversion services helped to define the central elements of Clarke American's future growth moves: a special focus on helping its partners find ways to grow their revenues and enhance their own customer relationships, and a readiness to play a direct role in helping banks manage those relationships.

Dawson explains this new focus: "We realized that we'd done a good job of keeping our bank customers happy. But what about *their* customers? Could we also make *them* happy? If we could, we knew it would make a big difference to our partners, because a happy customer is a lot easier to retain and grow. So we started focusing our efforts on new ways to not only take out waste but also to improve the end customer experience."

The Voice of the Customer

A new issue facing financial institutions, the emergence of telephone banking (and later Internet banking), represented the next opportunity for Clarke American. Traditionally, all new-check orders had been processed by customer service representatives in the local bank branch and then forwarded on to Clarke American. But customers increasingly liked the convenience of ordering directly by phone.

Not all financial institutions had the desire or ability to run call centers. At the same time, they could see the advantages of consolidating the check ordering function somewhere other than in the branch. Doing so would free up their staff to focus on more lucrative activities such as loan origination, and cut down on the inaccuracies created by handing off check information to the printer.

Clarke American responded by offering to take customer calls regarding all check ordering inquiries on behalf of its partners. This was a stretch for a check provider. But Clarke American was uniquely positioned to make such an offer, in part because it was early in developing real-time, online order entry and inquiry systems that could provide the backbone for the contact center operations.

In a way, this unique capability had grown out of Clarke American's roots and its culture of focusing relentlessly on operating efficiency. During the 1980s, the company had grown largely by purchasing small check printing businesses around the country. To help the company absorb these far-flung operations and improve capacity utilization, Clarke American created a single database linking all the plants. It was then a natural step to link this database into the systems run by the company's largest partners, which made automated data entry possible.

As financial institutions consolidated geographically, Clarke American's unified system became more and more advantageous—a powerful and unique hidden asset, in fact. Rather than having to track down a particular printing plant to ask about a check order, a bank employee could phone the company's regional customer service centers and get the information immediately. And over time, these contact centers had developed significant expertise in handling check printing inquiries with special efficiency.

Now Clarke American could use its contact centers to begin offering direct handling of customer check printing orders, without any work on the part of a bank employee. The company had earned the trust of its financial institution partners because of the way it had treated their employees when they called to place an order or make an inquiry. Clarke American measured the satisfaction levels for these interactions and could share them with the banks, providing an opening to discuss how it might provide the same level of service combined with careful performance measurement for their own customers.

Clarke American was now not just helping its partners better serve their customers, but in fact taking on this role directly. The contact centers operate around the clock and are staffed by highly trained customer service consultants focused solely on handling check orders. Mail and Internet contact channels are maintained as well. The scale and focus that the company brings to the task can create striking efficiency and quality gains for the bank.

Clarke American now runs several contact centers handling nine million direct customer inquiries and over six million orders per year for its partner banks. The company's role is invisible to the customer, as consultants answer the phone on behalf of the partner. Customers are much more satisfied than with the service typically provided by financial institutions because the consultants are experts in check product issues. Dawson recalls the results of one bank's switch to Clarke American:

> Some of our larger partners had developed algorithms that showed exactly how improving customer satisfaction increases revenue. When we started handling telephone inquiries for these partners, we told them, "We want you to measure customer satisfaction and track how well we do." And we insisted that they use the same tracking system that they'd used to measure their own performance previously. When they concluded their

studies, they showed that customer satisfaction, which was already high, had registered double-digit gains after we took over the programs.

More important, by running the contact centers, Clarke American helps its partners increase their check revenue, because its consultants are carefully trained to work with customers and upsell them to personalized checks and cross-sell accessories such as leather checkbook covers as appropriate. Clarke American and the bank share the profits realized from this upselling and cross-selling.

Clarke American recognizes that running the contact centers strengthens its role as a strategic partner in addition to generating new service fees and profit-sharing opportunities. At the same time, the company is building an important new hidden asset that will help fuel future growth: a direct connection to the end consumers and increasing insight into their banking habits. As Korbell puts it, "If you're not talking to the customer, someone else is. Having that direct link gives us an opportunity to increase satisfaction and loyalty for our partners."

And this new asset is now providing Clarke American with still more opportunities to build its business. For instance, the contact centers run a program they call "voice of the customer." The consultants record comments that reflect customer "delights and complaints" in a database that is available to the bank partner as well as to Clarke American employees companywide.

As Korbell explains, the voice-of-the-customer

program fills a growing challenge that most financial institutions face: "In the past, everyone worked together in the same building. The manager could walk out of his or her office and ask the customer reps, 'What's going on today?' Now, with the branches and the call centers and the headquarters all in different places, financial institutions need a system to capture and disseminate the same information."

The voice-of-the-customer program alerts Clarke American to opportunities and problems that its partners may not recognize. "One time, a partner's automated call response system went down," Korbell recalls. "We helped them pick this up quickly through our voice-of-the-customer program. We alerted the partner, and they were able to fix the system promptly."

The innovation doesn't stop there. Clarke American's latest generation of digital printing technology has given the company the capability to include customized messages in each check box, providing another tool to support partners in building stronger relationships with their own customers.

Clarke American has also harnessed its growing customer insight to help its partners improve customer retention. For example, a major cause of bank customer defections is moving from one home to another. At one time, it might have been necessary to change banks when you moved, since most banks were locally based. Today, however, with regional and national bank chains, there's often no real reason to change banks when you move. Yet many banks don't focus on retaining such customers.

In response, Clarke American will soon pilot a change-of-address offering for its partners. When Clarke American gets a check change-of-address request from a customer (often the first hint of an impending move), it will respond on behalf of the bank, sending along a free order of address labels or some other accessory, a coupon for a discounted banking service, and a message welcoming them to their new home. "This new product will create another opportunity for us to help our partners retain and grow revenue—a tremendous value for them," Korbell explains.

Clarke American is now putting in place its next step into the world of customer management solutions. For two pilot partners, the company is handling *all* inquiries and requests related to customers' checking accounts, including balance transfers, stop payments, and check tracking. In one sense, this is a natural evolution of the role that Clarke American has been playing for the past five years; in another, it is a bold new step. The company will be managing all aspects of the most important and central relationship between a financial institution and its customers—the checking account—and performing this task will require sharing sensitive account information with Clarke American.

The goal of these pilots is not just to shift this task to Clarke American. Ultimately, Clarke American will use customers' account information, flashed on the consultant's screen in real time, to make suggestions about new financial products and services the customer might be interested in. In addition to further strengthening relationships with partners and their customers, Clarke American hopes to share in the new value created.

Disciplined Innovation

Clarke American's success in building its new-growth business would be impossible without a strong commitment to service and product quality. In 2001, the company received the prestigious Malcolm Baldrige National Quality Award, and in 2002 Comerica, one of Clarke American's biggest partners, selected the firm as one of its five National Quality Excellence suppliers. These honors highlight an important focus for Clarke American and a common characteristic of most successful growth innovators. They bring quality and operating discipline not only to their base businesses but to their growth initiatives as well, combining creativity with a careful focus on measured implementation and consistent quality.

Dawson puts it this way: "If you want to have a conversation about handling the customer's contact with the bank, it's important that you focus on printing the checks right first."

When you excel in quality, your credibility with clients goes way up. Clarke American's leaders are now regularly invited by financial institutions to consult on their operational challenges and the development of high standards of service excellence. The goal in these exchanges is to create a common platform for joint strategic and operational planning with partners. Dawson explains: "A really successful and productive partner relationship is one where we can sit together with the management team and map out a set of joint objectives, performance improvement targets, and an action plan and timetable for getting it all done. If you can do that, you are a true strategic partner."

This emphasis on operating discipline permeates the company's approach to innovation as well. Its creativity is grounded in fact-based analysis, not random experimentation. "Many people think that as you go into a new area, you have to give up discipline," comments Korbell. "Actually, the opposite is true. The discipline is what allows you to go there."

The company's strategic planning process exemplifies its disciplined approach to growth and innovation. Working with the framework of a ten-year vision, the company leaders work together on a regular schedule to map three-year strategic plans and one-year goal deployment plans, with clearly defined roles, accountabilities, and time lines. The system ensures that daily activities within each operating unit are aligned with the company's long-term growth objectives, and, most importantly, that growth plans consistently turn into action.

Taking a Page from Clarke American's Playbook

Clarke American's new-growth surge began in a time of acute crisis. Yet the financial pressures of the mid-'90s really haven't subsided. Korbell says, "We're in a zero-sum game in this industry, with gale-force winds around us: declining prices, declining check use, increased use of debit cards and credit cards, and so on. It's like we start every year needing to grow by 4 percent just to keep from falling behind. So we *have* to be creative to find ways to better serve our partners and their customers."

Clarke American's creativity has paid off. By expanding its offerings from simple check printing into a broad array of bank services, the company has enlarged its potential market space from some $1.8 billion to $14 billion—an eightfold increase.

By viewing check printing and end customer management as a *system* of integrated services, Clarke American has grown its revenues in a declining market from $280 million in 1995 to $470 million today. And it has held its operating margins constant in the high teens, even as its core check printing business has faced increasing pressure.

Korbell sums it up this way: "We had to create a big vision to grow the business. And then we couldn't skip a step. We couldn't go from being a check printer to being a customer management solutions provider immediately. We had to earn our way by winning the trust of the financial institutions. When we help them with tough issues, it gives us the opportunity to create partnerships for life. And that's how the business grows."

Here are some questions to get you started in considering the potential of your company to build a similar growth program:

- Clarke American gave itself a big early boost by building an effective strategic customer program. Do you have such a program? If so, is it effective at developing increased revenues and uncovering emerging needs? If not, should you be developing one to better serve your important customers?
- Clarke American was particularly successful when it focused on its partners' customers. How well do you know the needs of your customers' customers? What can you do to help your customers serve those needs better? What opportunities do you have to interact directly with your customers' customers?
- Clarke American's systematic program for planning, deploying, and reviewing innovations significantly increases the chances for success of its new-growth initiatives. How disciplined is your own approach? How can your company begin building a similar process for encouraging and managing disciplined innovation?

7

"Our Biggest Wow!":
John Deere Landscapes

Thanks to its heritage as a manufacturer of tractors, lawn mowers, and other equipment, Deere & Company has great authority with landscapers, lawn contractors, and others who develop and maintain green spaces. Deere thought it saw an opportunity to build on this authority by launching a new business selling landscaping materials to green industry professionals. But given Deere's strong engineering and manufacturing tradition, what could it bring to an offshoot with such a strikingly different business model?

Serving "Those Who Work and Shape the Land"

Deere & Company was founded in 1837 by Illinois blacksmith John Deere, who'd created an innovative design for steel-bladed plows especially adapted to

Midwestern soil conditions. Visit Deere's Moline headquarters and you'll be impressed by the huge, gleaming tractors and combines on display—as well as historical plows, cultivators, tractors, and planters that made the Midwest the world's breadbasket. Still the leading producer of agricultural equipment, Deere also manufactures equipment for use in related fields such as construction, forestry, and lawn care—all designed to serve, in Deere's words, "those who work and shape the land."

Throughout Deere's history, the company's fortunes have been largely tied to the economics of agriculture, one of the world's most sharply cyclical industries. During the 1990–1992 farm recession, for example, Deere's revenues dropped 12 percent and profits practically disappeared.

Like other manufacturers in cyclical industries, Deere has been working continuously to improve its production efficiencies in pursuit of better and more stable earnings growth. But cost-cutting efforts will not suffice. Growth is also an important factor in continued success.

A natural place for Deere to look was within its Commercial and Consumer Equipment Division (C&CE), which makes lawn mowers, turf care equipment, and "gators" (heavy-duty utility carts). C&CE represented only about one-quarter of Deere's 2001 equipment sales of $11 billion, but the green industry it serves is growing much faster than either agriculture or construction, enjoying an estimated 10 to 15 percent annual growth.

The local contractor who mows lawns, the landscaper who designs and installs trees and shrubbery to beautify a new condo development, the company that tends the fairways at the nearby golf club, and the firm that installs and maintains sprinkler systems to keep the college campus blooming are all part of the green industry.

While green industry pros are all potential buyers of Deere's equipment, they also need huge amounts of plants and planting materials, consumables such as fertilizer, mulch, plant foods and pesticides, irrigation gear, lawn maintenance supplies, and other products. All in all, the green market amounts to $100 billion per year, five times as great as the $20 billion equipment market that C&CE was already serving.

What's more, green industry fundamentals look promising for the long term. As the baby boomers age, they are increasingly buying or building large, elaborate homes complemented by attractive landscaping. Awareness of and concern for the natural environment is widespread, and regulations concerning water use and landscaping are proliferating. For example, many communities have established rules about plantings: If a developer cuts down twenty trees to make room for new houses, twenty new ones must be planted later. And water-use restrictions put a premium on smart, efficient irrigation and sprinkling systems.

Taken together, these trends spell continued growth in the green industry business for years to come, and the broader possibilities looked intriguing.

Finding the Handle

To sort out exactly where and how to play in this landscape, C&CE president John Jenkins asked Dave Werning, then head of business development for the division, and Mike McGrady, a recently hired veteran of the irrigation industry, to explore the opportunity more closely. Over the course of several months, Werning and McGrady studied a series of potential entry points into the broader green industry market.

One idea in keeping with Deere's history was to get into the manufacture of irrigation equipment— pumps, sprinklers, control boxes, and other gear needed to supply water for landscapes ranging from home gardens to golf courses. This was a fast-growing business, and no one knew equipment manufacturing better than Deere.

Deere investigated different approaches, such as buying one of the larger manufacturers in the field, or acquiring several smaller companies. However, neither approach would deliver the magnitude of growth that Jenkins and Werning were aiming for.

What about fertilizer manufacturing, or running the nurseries that grow trees, shrubs, and ornamental plants for landscaping? Fertilizer manufacturing is dominated by huge commodity chemical companies, while nurseries require huge investments in land. Deere decided it wasn't interested in a big chemicals or real estate play.

What about looking downstream and becoming installers or maintainers of landscaping? The key to that field would be labor management. Deere would have to learn how to recruit, train, and manage a huge, geographically far-flung, low-cost, high-turnover labor force, one that was very different from the technically skilled, engineering-oriented manufacturing force it currently employed. Deere executives recognized that the pursuit of new growth might require changes in the company's management style and culture, but that particular shift seemed a step too far.

Taking another direction, Werning and McGrady began to focus on the structure of the green industry itself. When they did, they noticed that it was shaped like an hourglass. At the bottom are the landscapers, irrigation installers, and lawn maintenance companies—a highly fragmented business with few big players and tens of thousands of small operations. All these firms currently have to deal with products from thousands of suppliers at the top of the hourglass, including nurseries that grow trees, ornamental shrubs, and other plants; quarries that provide paving stone and other hard materials; and many small manufacturers of irrigation tubing, pipes, pumps, and other supplies.

The pinchpoint at the middle of the hourglass is distribution. While relatively more concentrated than either the suppliers or the small contractors themselves, the distribution business that connects them is still relatively fragmented, dominated by regional and local operations, as well as specialists who focus on narrow product subsets. Werning and McGrady began to consider whether launching a national company to consolidate and improve this link in the industry value chain might offer the growth opportunity they'd been seeking.

A few calculations showed that an all-in-one distribution company could claim a share of 50 percent of every dollar spent on a landscaping project. Consider a typical irrigation job: installing sprinklers on a homeowner's lawn, which might cost the consumer $2,500 or so. Fifty percent of that price would go to labor; the rest would go to equipment (sprinkler heads, pumps, control boxes, and so on) and to various materials (pipes, fittings, sod) which a distributor would provide.

Participating in half of a fast-growing $100 billion business looked to Deere like a significant opportunity. And this wasn't a low-margin business like distribution in many other industries. Landscape materials have relatively rich wholesale gross margins (as high as 40 percent for some items) and rapid inventory turnover as well.

Furthermore, Deere could see that there was real potential to create value for the green contractors over and above the product offerings. Because of the fragmented nature of distribution, many landscapers must spend hours every week traveling among various suppliers for the products they need, looking for current information about industry trends and regulations, tracking down unique plants or decorative items and juggling numerous financial accounts.

An integrated Deere distributor could provide the landscapers with one-source convenience and, by bundling in additional services, transform the landscape supply store from a traditional transaction-oriented supplier to a comprehensive business partner focused on improving the economics of the contractor.

The Dollar Value of Customer Authority

By mid-2000, Werning, McGrady, and Jenkins were seriously mulling the notion of entering the landscape distribution business. But for Deere & Company, with its proud heritage as a global, technically advanced manufacturer of agricultural and construction equipment, the idea of going into the distribution business to sell small, relatively simple and inexpensive products was a new and uncharted direction.

This was especially true in the late 1990s. It was the height of the e-business craze, and the conventional wisdom was that "Distribution is dead." So it would take guts to propose that Deere get into the distribution business.

There was one element of the opportunity, however, that gradually heightened the interest of Deere and raised their comfort level. Expanding its offerings to the green industry could leverage one of the firm's key hidden assets—its customer authority in this space. If that asset could be used to significantly enhance the economics of the distribution business, it might—just might—be enough to turn the proposition into a great new business.

Deere's "leaping deer" logo and green tractor are

known and trusted universally in the marketplace. They symbolize more than a century of innovative engineering and rugged construction in agriculture equipment and lawn tractors. But the halo of expertise extends into the green market more broadly. Thanks to its long history of technical innovation in agriculture and horticulture, Deere is viewed as knowing how plants grow and how to make them flourish. Drawing on this presumed expertise, Deere could have unique credibility and license to create a new bundle of green industry products, services, and distribution points.

This authority could produce tangible economic benefits for the new business. Customer acquisition costs would be lower for Deere than for a potential competitor, because it wouldn't have to spend as much to establish its name and induce customers to try its services. Deere's customer authority might also enable premium pricing on select products. And the company could create advertising and marketing efficiencies relative to competitors by promoting one name in all locales and across all product categories rather than diffusing its efforts among lots of small distributor names. Finally, the Deere team reasoned, the deepening of their customer relationships through the expansion into new-product lines might also benefit the core equipment business.

The Green Light

Pondering the potential of the Deere name, the C&CE team slowly went from hesitant to excited about the distribution opportunity. Approval by Deere's top executives was the next step. It helped that Werning was a longtime Deere employee with a strong financial background and credibility with Deere's senior managers. The fact that Jenkins's business had enjoyed a recent track record of success helped, too. But what clinched the deal was the strong support of Bob Lane, Deere's newly promoted chairman and CEO. Lane understood the urgent need for growth, and he recognized the potential in the green industry. In late 2000, Deere & Co. made the decision to go ahead, launching a new company named John Deere Landscapes (JDL). Werning and McGrady were put in charge.

For real success, though, support (or at least acceptance) for the initiative would also be required from the group that most directly served as the custodians of Deere's customer relationships: the network of John Deere dealers. Like many independent retailers, the dealers were living through tremendous change in their business. This made them skittish about anything that sounded like a potential new upheaval in distribution.

Werning and his colleagues understood that the dealers' concerns needed to be forthrightly addressed and managed. They soon realized that one of the additional advantages in focusing on the distribution of materials and irrigation equipment was that it would allow Deere to forge a direct relationship with customers. In fact, if done right, the move might actually create new ways to promote and reinforce the equipment dealers.

The Business Design Moves

Partially in response to the concerns of the John Deere dealer network, JDL sought to establish a very different relationship with its customers than the traditional Deere dealer would have. Landscapers may visit their Deere dealer to look at mowers or tractors once or twice a year. But a John Deere Landscapes store that sold plants and mulch and fertilizer might attract those same landscapers four times a week. One key to success for JDL would be maximizing those visits, then effectively managing customers' connections to the rest of Deere.

In order to quickly turn this vision into reality, Deere purchased two leading distributor chains. In January 2001, it acquired McGinnis Farms, a landscaping materials wholesaler. Headquartered in a suburb of Atlanta, McGinnis had fifty service centers in ten states and was a major distributor of nursery stock, landscaping materials, and irrigation supplies, including mulch, stone, soil, turf, gravel, pumps, hoses, fertilizer, and plants. The McGinnis stores are sprawling properties, often ten to twenty acres in size, with greenhouses, outdoor displays of trees and shrubs, and indoor stores filled with landscaping gear of all kinds.

Then, in October 2001, Deere acquired Richton International, an irrigation equipment distributor based in Michigan. Through its 160-plus Century Rain Aid locations, Richton was the nation's largest distributor of irrigation supplies, as well as equipment for outdoor lighting.

Deere combined these acquisitions into a single offering under one roof, building the capacity to offer single-source convenience for landscapers. They could now buy in a single location virtually all the supplies and equipment needed for any landscaping job, from trees to turf to gravel to pumps to lighting to fertilizer.

Werning and his team took care to make the transition seamless. For about four months after the McGinnis acquisition, JDL didn't even change the name of the business, and most if not all of the McGinnis managers and salespeople were kept on staff and in place. Many customers didn't even realize there had been a change until the new signs went up.

Deere's authority with customers played an important positive role. When the familiar green-and-yellow leaping deer logo began to appear on JDL storefronts, it evoked reactions of respect and even affection. George Wolf, a McGinnis store manager who is now a regional manager with JDL, sums it up nicely: "If McGinnis had to get acquired by somebody, John Deere was the best choice. Most of the contractors I sell to weren't upset when they heard about the deal. They just asked, 'So when can I get ahold of a John Deere hat?' "

"I'll Take That Any Time"

As Werning, McGrady, and Jenkins had envisioned, the combination of products and skills now offered under the umbrella of John Deere Landscapes makes it an attractive, convenient source for green industry contractors. But there was another major opportunity the team soon recognized: providing consumer credit to support their contractor customers.

In talking to contractors, JDL recognized that consumers often cut the size of landscaping projects or never undertook them because the project ended up being too large for their budget. Because they are small businesses, most landscapers are unable to offer their customers extended financing to spread out the financial burden.

So JDL took advantage of an important additional asset, one whose value it hadn't reckoned on when it first ventured into distribution: the John Deere Credit Division. As a major equipment finance company, John Deere Credit has more than five hundred thousand accounts and a managed asset portfolio of nearly $13 billion.

Working with John Deere Credit, JDL put together a financing program, including installment credit and sales tools such as instant online approval, that loyal JDL contractors can offer to their landscaping clients. An installer in the program can visit the prospective client, explain how John Deere Credit works, and say, "Let's dial in with my laptop and get you approved for credit right away." In a few minutes, the landscaper can say, "Gee, you're going to have such a beautiful landscape when we're done with the installation. How about adding some outdoor lighting so you can enjoy it in the evening as well? Your new credit line will make it affordable."

In this way, landscaper revenues grow, and more green product purchases flow through to JDL, while relationships are strengthened between the consumer and landscaper and between the landscaper and Deere.

Carroll Howell, president of Howell Landscaping, a JDL customer in Georgia, appreciates the power of John Deere Credit to enhance his business. "When we cost out an entire landscape plan, many customers don't necessarily do the entire plan," Howell explains. "They'll do part this year, part next year, part the next." This is far from ideal from Howell's perspective. Not only does it stretch out the cash flow, but work delayed is sometimes work forgotten or forgone. John Deere Credit changes the equation for Howell's customers. "This program lets them do it all right now—and many are doing that," he says.

For Howell Landscaping, the results have been impressive. In a typical recent month, the company took in $90,000 worth of sales financed by John Deere Credit ("a big portion of our total base"), and these contracts averaged 36 percent larger than the average noncredit sale. "I'll take that any time," Howell remarks. In 2002, Howell's sales were up

16 percent, and his profits up 20 percent, a strong performance he attributes largely to John Deere Credit.

Once a homeowner's project is completed, he will be given a JDL credit card, facilitating future purchases. And since homeowners who are interested in maintaining and enhancing their grounds are historically excellent credit risks, the possibility of financial loss is lower than for the average home loan.

In time, the availability of John Deere Credit should help fuel further growth of the green industry. Think about Carroll Howell's story, then multiply it thousands of times. That is the economic power of the JDL business design.

In the first two months after the March 2002 launch of this new business, JDL signed up 350 contractors to offer John Deere Credit to their customers. No wonder Dave Werning calls the new availability of John Deere Credit to JDL customers "our biggest Wow! of the year."

Beyond Credit

The consumer credit success offered a powerful lesson for the JDL team: Some of the best opportunities to serve new customer needs only become apparent once you are working closely with them. JDL is using this lesson to look for more ways to provide innovative services for its customers.

One of those ways is by increasingly serving as a

business adviser to its customers, assisting with design and planning concepts, especially in the irrigation field. This isn't a formal process but more a matter of grabbing a piece of paper and sketching out some ideas for a customer. But JDL's staff brings a lot of expertise to this role, which significantly enhances the customer connection. JDL also helps train its customers through seminars. In Texas, where irrigation installers must be licensed, JDL conducts qualifying classes and offers follow-on programs that are eligible for continuing education credit.

JDL is now working on fresh ideas to further enhance the economics of its customers—for example, by passing along customer leads generated by JDL advertising to local contractors in JDL's partners program.

Of course, the company also benefits in a variety of ways. First, JDL contributes new growth and revenue stability. By offering a wide array of products and services under one roof, JDL enjoys a diverse revenue stream that helps smooth out the cyclical variation that plagues manufacturers of costly capital goods.

JDL also now has access to a much larger share of customer activity than that enjoyed by the traditional John Deere equipment dealer. And since JDL is the largest player in the green industry, it should enjoy significant scale advantages including bargaining clout with its suppliers, an accelerated ramp-up of the business, and the ability to market, advertise, and promote on a large scale.

Negotiating the Dealer Relationship

Werning and his team are looking for ways to leverage the success of John Deere Landscapes to the benefit of the traditional Deere equipment dealers and the core Deere business. Some of the methods they're testing are small-scale and informal. JDL store managers hold cookouts where they bring their customers together with the John Deere dealers, they put on trade shows where Deere dealers display and explain their products, and they send account managers to travel with dealers to call on customers.

Some John Deere equipment is on display in the JDL stores. A few small items are sold directly; JDL stores hold racks of backpack blowers, string trimmers, and the like. And there's a direct phone connection to the John Deere dealer so that a customer's question about buying a tractor or mower can be answered immediately.

Much trickier is the notion of physically co-locating the John Deere dealer and the JDL store. Deere equipment dealerships are small and ideally located in high-traffic areas to catch browsers and comparison shoppers. JDL sites are much larger and tend to be visited as destinations for specific items. So JDL likes locations on the outskirts of growing communities, where land is plentiful and less expensive and where the landscapers are busy working on new developments. But the John Deere dealer wants to be near the commercial center. This poses a conundrum for co-locating stores that JDL is still tinkering with.

Fortunately, because of the preparation and communication done early in the process, most of the Deere dealers are buying into the JDL concept. A few early success stories help—like the tale of the Deere dealer who could never get a return call from the local contractor whose equipment business he coveted. The contractor started buying his supplies from JDL, which arranged an introduction to the Deere dealer, who soon sold him $80,000 worth of machinery.

As stories like this circulate on the company grapevine, the worries of the equipment dealers are gradually diminishing. JDL has learned that with creative attention from management, the potential liability of channel conflict can be transformed into an asset—the opportunity to develop and nurture a separate distribution channel that actually reinforces traditional outlets.

What's Ahead?

JDL still has far to go to combine Deere's capabilities with those of McGinnis and Century Rain Aid into a single powerful whole. For one thing, there are currently full-service JDL outlets in just a dozen U.S. states (concentrated in the South), so that geographic rollout across the country has just begun.

Many Century Rain Aid stores still sell irrigation supplies only. JDL is now gradually transforming them into full-concept stores offering all the supplies a landscape contractor is likely to need. There's good economic potential in this kind of expansion. Because only 25 percent of the typical project cost is irrigation equipment, $1 million in sales through Century Rain Aid for irrigation products could translate into $2 million to $4 million in sales for an expanded full-concept store.

JDL is also looking for new ways to expand the services it offers, building on its ever-expanding base of assets. Starting with Deere's authority in the green industry, JDL has added to its growth balance sheet the leading distribution channel, John Deere Credit, new insights about the economics of the landscaping business, and burgeoning customer relationships.

To take advantage of these assets, Werning is working to develop a tool for analyzing his customers' cost of doing business—labor, real estate, supplies, and so on—which will permit JDL to demonstrate specific levels of cost saving. And he talks about the possibility of expanding the John Deere Credit offerings to include commercial financing and home equity lines of credit.

JDL is meeting its profitability and return on assets targets. But the key question that Dave Werning is wrestling with is this: *What's the big Wow! for next year?*

Taking a Page from Deere's Playbook

If you help run a successful incumbent company, you can probably identify one or more groups of customers with whom your firm has significant authority. Your company might be able to build a new business that leverages that authority while meeting those customers' next-generation needs. Here are some questions to jump-start your thinking about this opportunity.

- John Deere realized that it had authority with customers that transcended its product offering. Where does your company have customer authority that is going unused? Are there customer segments that you underserve or don't serve at all that are likely to be receptive to an innovative offer from your company?
- One of Deere's biggest successes was in helping customers grow their own revenues through credit. How can you help your customers grow their revenues? Do you have unique financing, brokering, or other skills that might help?
- Deere initially worried about channel conflict. Are there similar concerns that hold you back from new initiatives? If so, are there creative ways to manage or work around these liabilities so as to transform them into new kinds of assets?

8

"Honing Innovation to a Fine Art": Johnson Controls

Trapped in a world of large, powerful customers and commodity price pressures, Johnson Controls has turned its position as an automobile seat manufacturer into a powerful platform for new growth. From assembling seats a decade ago to developing entire automotive subsystems today, the company is pursuing a goal of reducing the structural inefficiencies in the automotive industry. How has Johnson Controls managed to make this transition and create consistent double-digit revenue and profit growth in such a tough situation?

Condition Red

June 3, 1992. The mere mention of the date is enough to send shivers down the spine of any American auto parts maker. On that day, nearly six hundred suppliers were gathered for a meeting with GM's fiery purchasing czar, Ignacio Lopez de Arriortua. As Lopez prepared to speak, unease permeated the convention hall. The year before, GM had posted a record $4.5 billion loss, prompting the firing of its president and its chief financial officer. Against that backdrop, no good news was expected.

Lopez did not disappoint. He laid down the law: GM intended to slash the $50 billion it spent each year on parts and raw materials. In North America, nearly all of GM's supplier contracts would be torn up and fresh bids would be solicited. Those in the room who couldn't lower their prices would be cut loose.

Among the assembled suppliers, the reaction was something close to panic. Everyone understood that the Big Three automakers desperately needed to cut costs. But the suppliers were feeling the pinch of a tight economy, too. To them, it sounded like GM was trying to get blood from a stone. And everyone knew just how hard the behemoth could squeeze.

But one group of supply-company executives kept their composure. Their expressions, in fact, betrayed something akin to satisfaction. Their company, Johnson Controls, Inc. (JCI), had been preparing for this situation for nearly a decade.

As most of GM's supplier base plunged into uncertainty and fear, Johnson was poised to enjoy yet another year of record growth.

New Frontiers

It's a mark of corporate excellence when a company is able to hold its own against numerous well-entrenched competitors. But when a company is able to consistently post double-digit growth in an otherwise stagnant industry where everyone else is struggling just to stay alive, that's nothing short of astonishing. And that's the Johnson Controls story.

Remarkably, JCI is a relative newcomer to the auto supply business. The Milwaukee-based company was founded in 1885 by Professor Warren Johnson, inventor of an early thermostat. By the middle of the twentieth century, the company had grown into a dominant player in the building controls field. Then, in 1985, it moved suddenly and aggressively into a new industry by purchasing Hoover Universal, which produced seating components for the domestic automobile industry. Hoover became the Automotive Supply Group of Johnson Controls.

JCI's new line of business turned out to be less attractive than expected. Retail sales of passenger cars in the United States were stagnant; in the decade after 1985, unit sales would fall from 15.4 million to 14.8 million per year. As a medium-sized supplier of seating components, Johnson was a low-margin contractor to an industry with dismal prospects.

Tough Times in Detroit

JCI's new business environment was riddled with massive, systemic inefficiencies driven by the industry's capital- and labor-intensive method for building components such as seats. Each of the Big Three designed and assembled its seats in-house, with components coming from many outside suppliers. At one point, Chrysler was assembling seats using parts produced by no fewer than twenty-six suppliers.

This system was wasteful in the best of times and financially punishing in bad times. All those employees, their machines, tools, and inventory represented a high fixed cost that dragged down profits whenever the business cycle entered a downturn. In the early 1980s, the cycle was definitely down. What's worse, the Big Three were losing market share as better-built, cheaper imports infiltrated the U.S.

The manufacturers needed to cut costs. But their fixed costs weren't going down—they were going up. Carmaking was becoming a more expensive and technologically challenging process, and the variety of models and trim levels was proliferating.

As choices broadened, so did the complexity of the cars. Electronics multiplied in the engine, the dashboard, and the passenger compartment. Rising consumer expectations in such areas as safety and fuel economy were producing ever-growing pressures that were often contradictory, since the easiest way to make a car safer is to make it *heavier*, wile the easiest way to make it more fuel-efficient is to make it *lighter.* Achieving acceptable levels of both while meeting design needs demanded razor-sharp engineering work.

To survive, the Big Three needed to accomplish three major objectives: reduce the fixed costs of their manufacturing, streamline their car design processes, and make their production systems more flexible and efficient. They had to do all this while dramatically broadening their range of choices available to consumers.

JCI realized it was situated to help automakers pursue these do-or-die goals. By viewing its market position as a unique hidden asset, the firm could turn its position in seating components into a launching pad for new growth moves.

Turning Japanese

One aspect of JCI's market position that created new growth opportunities was a distinctive relationship with Japanese automakers. This derived from a ball-bearing business that Hoover had owned prior to the JCI merger. When Nissan built the first Japanese-owned auto plant in the United States in the early 1980s, it chose Hoover as a supplier based on its success with Hoover as a ball-bearing supplier in Japan.

When other Japanese manufacturers arrived to build their own North American plants, JCI was first in line as a supplier. This created new revenue for

JCI, of course, but the Japanese connection was more important for a less obvious reason. In becoming a supplier to the Japanese, JCI had to learn a new way of doing business—one that would help the firm take the first step on its growth journey.

In Japan, automakers didn't bother to build their own major systems such as seats or gearboxes. Instead, they relied on a hierarchical system of suppliers. Large Tier One suppliers took delivery of parts from smaller Tier Two and Tier Three suppliers and assembled the systems for the automobile manufacturers. To serve its Japanese customers, then, JCI had to move from making components to assembling complete seats, a role that added more value. As a supplier to Japanese OEMs, Johnson also needed to become adept at lean production and just-in-time delivery techniques that boosted flexibility and slashed inventory costs.

Soon building seats for the Japanese became a mainstay for Johnson. The result was a head start in developing broader assembly and integration skills that few of its competitors shared. One by one, domestic manufacturers began coming to JCI for seat assembly. Like the Japanese, they saw the advantage of reducing their fixed costs by letting suppliers shoulder the payroll, equipment, and capital costs of component manufacturing and assembly. American automakers also saw that JCI's specialization allowed it higher production efficiency than they themselves could attain.

However, JCI soon saw that it wasn't taking full advantage of the opportunities in seating. Its foam and metal frames made up only a quarter of the value of a car seat. The rest of the components, from seat covers to mechanical and electronic posture controls, had to be sourced from other suppliers. In many cases, these suppliers were chosen by the car manufacturers, reducing JCI's ability to improve the system and to capture margin on the other components. As a result, the business amounted to processing materials with low-cost labor, a good first move but an inherently limited role with scant opportunities for long-term revenue or profit growth.

JCI devoted the rest of the 1980s to changing all that.

To enhance its capability to produce entire car seats, JCI moved quickly to acquire companies and start up new joint ventures in rapid succession: Ferro Manufacturing Corporation, a maker of seat tracks and recliner mechanisms (acquired in 1985); Techno Trim and Trim Masters, manufacturers of seat covers (launched in 1986 and 1988, respectively); and AG Simpson, a maker of manual seat tracks (acquired in 1988). By the end of the decade, JCI had the technical skills and plant capacity to design and produce all the major components of an automobile seat.

To the Drawing Board

Now that the company was producing complete seats, its next goal was to add seat design capabilities so that it could further increase the value it provided to customers. Here again, JCI's chief hidden asset—its market position—conferred a unique advantage. Of all the components and systems in a car, seats were singularly well suited to delegating design responsibility from an auto manufacturer to an independent supplier. A door, dashboard module, or overhead assembly must fit seamlessly into the nearby parts. But seats are different. "Seats are a pretty distinct subsystem," says Paul Dickensheets, JCI's vice president and general manager, Integrated Interiors. "That's the beauty of it. They can be assembled almost independently from the rest of the car."

In addition, seats represent a unique balance between simplicity and complexity. Because carmakers did not view seats as a critical value-added point of differentiation, such as the power train or overall styling, they were willing to consider outsourcing seat design before other components. Yet seats are valuable and reasonably complicated—the single most expensive component of an interior, which in turn is the most expensive part of a car. Their high price tag would justify significant research and development expenditures. Had JCI served another part of the market—for example, making valves and other engine parts like Eaton—pursuring ownership of an entire subsystem probably would have been impossible. Seats were *just complicated and important enough* to serve as the strategic platform.

The challenge was finding a carmaker willing to delegate design responsibility for a major subsystem to its supplier. But by the late 1980s, JCI could see that the U.S. manufacturers were no longer monolithic in their thinking. Chrysler, in particular, was willing to explore new ways of working with suppliers. On the brink of bankruptcy a few years before, only to be saved by a congressional bailout and the introduction of the minivan, Chrysler executives knew they needed still more innovative solutions to reclaim their position in the marketplace.

As the smallest of the Big Three, Chrysler had the most to gain by outsourcing engineering, development, and production costs. By taking on the complete design and assembly role, JCI could help Chrysler lower the overall cost of the seat by integrating components, reducing the number of parts, designing it for easy assembly, and reducing the wasteful back-and-forth between designers and manufacturing engineers in the development process. Knowing it could accomplish this goal, JCI began aggressively courting Chrysler.

An important part of this courtship involved shifting JCI's attention to a new set of buyers within the OEM. As a component supplier, JCI had traditionally sold to the purchasing department. When it moved into just-in-time assembly, it had learned how to sell to manufacturing engineers and plant managers. Now the company had to go still higher in the organization and move earlier in the development process, forging relationships with design engineers and vehicle platform executives.

JCI also needed to learn the unique concerns felt by these new decision makers. They cared most about design cycle-time reduction and the technical performance of the seats. JCI's traditional strengths in component cost and production reliability were secondary concerns for them. These customers also viewed the seat as a system of trade-offs that had to be managed in order to hit a target production cost.

The company's efforts bore fruit in 1989 when Chrysler asked for help in designing seats for the Neon, a follow-on to the Sundance/Shadow line of compacts. "It was a matter of survival," recalls Jim Geschke, JCI's vice president and general manager, Electronics Integration. "They needed to make their supply base leaner. We helped them reinvent their development model."

From Adversaries to Partners

The move to seating system supplier did not go smoothly at first. Problems began with negotiations around the target cost of JCI's seats. Initially, the company proposed a price per seat of $450. Unknown to JCI, Chrysler's target price was $330. The gap suggested significantly different views of what the seat specifications would be.

Both sides were upset, each believing it had been misled by the other. Both were stuck in the framework of a traditional outsourcing relationship in which a customer would deliver specs to a supplier who would then offer a negotiable quote. Each side would try hard to maneuver in pursuit of the best possible price. The relationship was essentially adversarial.

If JCI was going to take on the broader and deeper set of responsibilities entailed in designing seats for Chrysler, that relationship would have to change. The company would need to understand Chrysler's internal deadlines, design criteria, and budgeting requirements and become a true economic partner. Eager to prevent the opportunity from slipping away, JCI quickly cobbled together a team representing every department of the company and sent it to study the Chrysler operation. "We learned more about Chrysler in three months than we had in five years," one manager recalls. "And we learned about our own efforts internally and what it took to get something done. We found new ways of doing business . . . and within three months, we took one hundred dollars off the cost of that seat by *jointly* defining the most important design requirements."

The deal went through, and JCI had learned an important lesson: When customer readiness threatens to block a new-growth initiative, finding and nurturing a single customer with special reasons to expand the business relationship may lead to the necessary breakthrough.

In the end, the Neon was a hit. Chrysler credited JCI as a major factor in the vehicle's success, and together the two companies had pioneered a new kind of vendor–supplier partnership. The approach required a lot of trust on both sides and a willingness to live with a degree of ambiguity concerning the final terms of the business agreement. But in the end, the partnership created unprecedented value for both parties.

For Chrysler, this took the form of better, cheaper seats produced more efficiently and with far fewer design and manufacturing headaches for its own employees.

For JCI managers, the success of the Chrysler project—especially when contrasted with the maelstrom of supplier relationships at GM—pointed the way to a more attractive future as an auto supplier. JCI could now expand beyond the traditional purchasing model, in which many small, fragmented suppliers scrambled to sell parts to a handful of powerful, monolithic automakers. Instead, it could pursue contracts for complete seating systems that provided greater value for customers and improved margins for itself. Soon, other automakers were following Chrysler's lead and ceding greater responsibility for seat design to JCI.

Testing, Testing

November 1994. Inside a sealed laboratory in Plymouth, Michigan, technicians strap a pair of life-sized dummies into a mock-up of a vehicle passenger compartment mounted on a powerful high-G-force-generating sled. The technicians retreat behind a safety barrier as a siren's deafening blare fills the room. At the touch of a control room button, the sled rockets forward, slamming the mock-up into a concrete wall. With a tremendous crash, the vehicle compartment disintegrates, sending the mannequins flying and spraying the lab with fragments of twisted metal, plastic, and glass. In moments, technicians surround the wreckage, assessing the damage and looking for clues to be used in improving the design of seats, belts, harnesses, airbags, and the interior systems.

You've seen films of impact tests like these in advertisements by carmakers eager to boast of their vehicles' safety features. But this test took place at Johnson Controls' high-G test facility, unique among seating suppliers. "We are the first ones to do this," says Tony Kestian, JCI's director of business development, Seating. "It helped us develop credibility with our customers in the area of seating systems."

The emphasis on testing was part of JCI's next big move: from seating design to research and testing. Traditionally, when the firm got orders from its customers, the product specifications were already defined. No one expected the company to conduct its own basic research or to determine seating requirements. How could a supplier sink money into such pursuits and still compete on the all-important parameter of price?

But by the mid-1990s, the U. S. car industry was attuned to the value of lean production, demanding closer relationships with suppliers and handing them more responsibility in return. From 1980 to 1990, JCI had increased its R&D spending tenfold and had expanded its engineering staff to more than six hundred. Now it was designing and building more seats than any carmaker. The OEMs were beginning to ask: *Why have our own basic seat development when JCI's deep expertise and experience with basic seat architectures lets the company do it faster, cheaper, and better?*

JCI had also begun conducting its own consumer research to find out what drivers and passengers really wanted from auto seats, then translating those insights into new features. In the early 1990s, for instance, researchers learned about an intriguing phenomenon taking place across America. Parents with young children were hooking up television sets and VCRs in the back seats of their cars and minivans to keep tots occupied on long trips For sociologists, this represented an interesting cultural development; for JCI, it defined a new product niche. The firm leapt in, designing a TV-and-VCR unit built into the overhead panel. It was just the sort of thing automakers were looking for to help their products stand out from the herd—and car buyers loved the units. JCI now supplies millions of these units a year.

Building the Idea Factory

Despite a few early steps at expanding into new-business areas such as the VCR console, seating was still JCI's biggest moneymaker, and internal analysis predicted that growth in that market would end within less than ten years. Competitors had moved to take advantage of the same opportunities that had fed JCI's recent growth—entire seats designed and manufactured for just-in-time delivery. The company's head start was eroding.

A renewed price squeeze underscored the problem. "Seats were moving toward commodity status," says Dickensheets. "The automakers' mentality was, 'We paid $100 for them this year; next year we're going to pay $95.'" With margins shrinking, it wouldn't be enough to simply master the seating niche. New growth opportunities were needed.

One path, JCI decided, was to lay claim to other parts of the car interior, such as headliners, instrument panels, and flooring. These all suffered from the same problems that seating had a decade earlier: Manufacturers were still designing and producing them inefficiently in-house, buying parts from many small suppliers. Again, JCI's valuable hidden asset—its market position in seating—would play an important role.

For Johnson, not only did these components represent a huge potential market space that surrounded the seat, but they also interacted with the seat to create an "interior system" that was becoming increasingly important to discriminating buyers. Unfortunately, Johnson had no experience in any of these areas, and creating it from the ground up would be a lengthy and expensive process.

Opportunity came knocking in the form of an acquisition candidate. Prince Automotive, located in Holland, Michigan, was one of the most successful privately held auto supply firms, with expertise in lighting, visors, overhead consoles, ceiling supports, and other interior components. It also had a reputation for technical innovation and forward thinking. The company had hoped to grow into a major Tier One supplier, but it was hobbled by a lack of capital. When its founder died, his widow decided that the only way forward was a merger. JCI seized the chance.

The deal with Prince was done in 1996, with JCI paying $1.3 billion to acquire the firm. In one move, JCI became a serious, multiple-threat competitor in interiors. The jewel in the crown was a technology that Prince had been developing called HomeLink, which allowed a driver to control home lighting and security systems from inside the car using a radio-frequency transmitter-receiver. HomeLink transformed the mundane felt headliner in the roof of a car into a differentiated, high-value system. Here was the blueprint for future innovation that would embed new consumer functionality in otherwise nondescript interior pieces.

JCI also gained valuable new management skills from the acquisition. Prince had developed a dynamic and creative corporate culture that thrived on creating previously unimagined functionalities. This culture was now transplanted into Prince's new corporate parent. "Prince had honed innovation to a fine art," says Kestian. "Many of the processes used at Johnson Controls today originally came from Prince."

Now JCI's move along this second growth vector entered a new phase. It was no longer merely seizing existing real estate in the car parts business, like a Dutch reclamation engineer, it was creating *new* real estate.

In the wake of the Prince takeover, JCI embarked on a new series of acquisitions to round out its interior capabilities. In 1998, it acquired the German supplier Becker, which specialized in door systems, instrument panels, ceiling panels, and floor consoles. Two years later, it acquired Ikeda Bussan, a seating supplier that gave JCI a greater presence in Asia. The following year, JCI acquired Sagem, a French company specializing in instrument cluster, body and engine controls, and mobile communications. By 2001, JCI could build every part of the car interior, it had expanded into high-value electronics content, and it had significantly broadened its reach in Europe and Asia.

Recognizing that a steady flow of new ideas would be essential to its future success, JCI opened a 226,000-square-foot technology center in Plymouth, Michigan, in 1998, housing more than three hundred engineering and technology staff. This center is the home to JCI's Core Customer Research program, which studies real drivers and passengers in search of interior innovation ideas. For example, engineers run the Comfort Lab, a specialized facility that no carmaker can match (though Ford has started work on a similar unit). "The purpose of the Comfort Lab is to learn more about the occupant experience," says Elizabeth Spooner, JCI's director of worldwide strategic planning. "The goal is to identify the most important characteristics for each occupant of the car and to find ways to enhance their experience."

From data collected in the Comfort Lab, JCI has developed several significant new technologies, including Comfort Cools, which draws air through the seat to remove heat and moisture from an occupant's back and legs, and Comfort Renews, which rhythmically inflates and deflates air bladders inside the seat cushion to create a massaging up-and-down motion similar to walking.

With its high-G sled facility, JCI had undertaken the kind of basic research that had once been the province of the big automakers. Now it was delving deeper into the science and psychology of car interiors than anyone had ever ventured before. JCI was spending more than 3 percent of its sales on R&D, twice as much as its nearest competitor.

The auto industry was receptive to good new ideas. Widespread adoption of lean production technology meant that high levels of quality and reliability were no longer selling points. Consumers expected them. To differentiate their car models more effectively, automakers needed innovative products and functionalities that enhanced the consumer's enjoyment. That's exactly the challenge JCI was eager to meet.

Today, JCI conducts more customer research on interiors than any automaker. Using this data, the company is able to design interiors and interior products specifically targeted to certain market segments. TravelNote, an electronic product aimed at harried professionals, lets drivers record up to three minutes' worth of verbal memos. PlaySeat, created in cooperation with Lego, is a rear-seat child activity module that stores Legos and other toys, holds juice boxes and cups, and serves as a writing and play surface. JCI has even been able to help automakers respond to news events that change consumer preferences. For instance, when word of Firestone tire failures made headlines, JCI came to market with PSI, a radio-frequency device that relays real-time tire pressure data to a console-mounted readout.

GM Redux

The logical culmination of Johnson's two-directional expansion into design and the interior would be to integrate entire interiors, with Johnson assuming complete control over design, production, and sourcing. Such integration, Johnson has long felt, could help drive innovation while saving carmakers money.

Chrysler had been the breakthrough customer for the first expansion of JCI's business model. Ironically, it was GM—the company that had embodied old-school supplier relationships under Lopez—that played the same role this time. In 2002, GM awarded complete interior program management contracts for its new midsized car and minivan platforms to Johnson Controls. "Based on what Johnson has done over the years, we've decided that they're more expert in interiors than we are," says GM spokesman

Jim Parks. "They are more in tune with what consumers want. And they're in tune with the materials."

Coordinating the design and manufacture of the complete interior will enable JCI to improve the overall interior design in ways that otherwise would be impossible. "The traditional mind-set in the auto business is to select the best component manufacturer for each area," says Kestian. "While this allows you to get the best components, it doesn't optimize the overall design. For example, if you source a radio box and heating controls from two different suppliers, each will be in a self-contained module with individual walls. Putting them next to each other doubles the walls, taking up space and adding weight. A total system owner can remove this duplication."

It's clear that JCI now exists in a different world than it did fifteen years ago. "Before, automakers would basically give us a blueprint," says Johnson spokesman David Roznowski. "Now they look to us to make vehicles a better place for consumers to be."

Next Stop: The Future

"You have to have a vision of where you want to go," says Dickensheets. "Johnson has always had that vision six to eight years down the road."

JCI has grown by accurately perceiving its customers' needs—often before the customers do—and then lavishing resources on meeting those needs.

Whether it's building complete car seats for Toyota, designing seats for Chrysler, or integrating entire car interiors for GM, the company's willingness to invest ahead of the curve has consistently opened up lucrative new opportunities.

Looking ahead, there's still more value to capture within the realm of interior integration, Dickensheets says. "There are cars out there that have $4,000 worth of interior. That includes the steering column, the HVAC [heating, ventilating, and air-conditioning] system, the electrics, and the electronics. At present, we don't make all that stuff. But the $3,000 to $4,000 range is what I'd like for us to control. That's the magnitude of what we're looking for."

An important step in accessing more of that value will be controlling the selection of Tier Two and Tier Three suppliers. "That's going to be the next opportunity," Dickensheets predicts. "In our mind, if we were given that control, both we and the customer would win significantly. It would give us the opportunity to drive vendor selection and rationalization decisions from an overall interior product focus."

For example, at present a car that features remote keyless entry, HomeLink, and remote tire pressure sensing might have three radio-frequency transmitter-receivers, because a different group within the automaker sources each system. When Johnson provides the whole interior as an integrated system, it will offer the same functions with one unit at one-third the cost.

JCI is developing new interior systems that could continue to change both the ways automakers build cars and the ways consumers buy and use them. Interior prototypes have been built with features that can be mixed and matched to particular demographic niches. AdVenture, a concept minivan aimed at the "active lifestyle" consumer, comes equipped with a pullout bike rack, an onboard video entertainment system, and storage areas for sports gear. Concerto, a concept interior for seniors, provides controls that are closer together and easier to reach. With each of these innovations, JCI is anticipating and shaping the needs of the future, not just responding to the needs of today.

A few years from now, JCI envisions producing branded, replaceable modules that a dealer can change on demand and that consumers may buy more than one of. This would separate the seat purchase from the vehicle purchase and provide Johnson with still new customers, dealers, and end consumers. For instance, says Johnson Chairman and CEO James Keyes, "Dealers may take back a leased car that had two built-in seats for children and redo it with an interior designed by JCI for a single person."

Even further down the road, JCI expects that enormous opportunities will arise as electronic controls gain acceptance. Steer-by-wire, shift-by-wire, and brake-by-wire systems will radically redefine the relationship between the interior and the rest of the car. Sophisticated and aggressive integrators may find whole new horizons opening up.

"This is an exciting time for Johnson," says Dickensheets, "because we think there's a need there for what we do. It's a win–win situation—actually, win–win–win. We feel we can give the consumer a higher-quality interior, identify significant cost savings for the automaker, and continue to make money ourselves."

Looking back two decades to the beginnings of JCI's auto supply business, it's breathtaking to see how far the company has come. In 1985, it was essentially a foam-cutting operation, a cheap source of nonunion labor. By 2001, the operation had burgeoned into a $12-billion-a-year industry leader that is literally shaping the car interiors business. From previously garnering about $600 worth of content from each car, it now gets some $1,300. From capturing value only through simple component assembly, JCI now earns enhanced margins from taking on the assembly, design, and integration roles. As a result, the company's revenues, profits, and market capitalization have all shown sustained steady double-digit growth for the past decade, and it owns a bigger share of a bigger market than ever before.

Taking a Page from Johnson Controls' Playbook

The JCI story offers a number of lessons for company leaders who may feel trapped in a no-growth zone. Recognizing the opportunities afforded by a crucial hidden asset—a unique position in the automotive marketplace—JCI's executives used those opportunities to begin expanding the products and services they offered to customers, addressing an array of previously neglected next-generation needs, especially the inefficiencies inherent in the industry's old supplier model. The results were huge new benefits for customers and enormous, lucrative growth for JCI.

Can your company borrow a leaf or two from this playbook? Consider these questions:

- The economics of the automakers were deeply flawed by inefficiencies, redundancies, and excessive costs. JCI has grown by addressing these flaws. What are the flaws in your customers' economics? How can you help to address them?
- Are your company's efforts to expand offerings hampered by the unreadiness of customers to broaden your role in their business? If so, how can you identify and partner with a potential customer that has special reasons to be receptive, as Chrysler had?
- JCI has developed the asset base on which its growth is built through company acquisitions, internal growth, and alliances. Are there assets your company needs to take advantage of? If so, how can these be bought, grown, or developed through alliances?

9

"Customers Don't Care About Our R&D": Air Liquide

Technical know-how can be a powerful ally in getting closer to your customers. Capabilities that you consider commonplace may be capable of solving some of your customers' most difficult and costly conundrums. A decade ago, Air Liquide's powerful technical know-how stood largely untapped. The R&D capability that the company prided itself on was neither understood nor respected by its customers. How could this undervalued technical know-how become the key ingredient in developing a new-services business to address customers' next-generation needs and generate new growth?

Selling Air

Being a supplier of basic industrial materials is one of the toughest businesses on earth. Suppliers of such commodities have to invest in huge amounts of fixed assets, contend with cyclical swings in demand and prices, and protect their profits against fierce competition. In sectors such as metals, chemicals, and petroleum, there is little differentiation between one firm's products and another's, and there are few real technical breakthroughs that can propel firms to the forefront.

Moreover, basic materials suppliers are often poorly positioned to recognize and address the critical issues facing their customers. They sit far upstream from where value is created, and their customers often take them for granted. Once traditional growth moves such as geographic expansion and acquisitions have been exhausted, suppliers often face a grim future of highly cyclical revenues and profits, driven by swings in the overall economy.

Air Liquide is one of those special companies that has been able to reinvent its business design to create new value for its customers and new growth for itself in this unforgiving sector. A century-old, tradition-laden industrial gas company, Air Liquide has transformed itself by using its technical expertise in producing, distributing, and using gas in industrial settings—the know-how that customers had taken for granted—to address many critical operating issues facing its customers.

The Old Order: Nice While It Lasted

Air Liquide was founded in France in 1902 to sell gases to producers of steel, cars, and other industrial products. A pioneer in the use of cryogenic techniques to produce such gases as oxygen and nitrogen, Air Liquide has continued to refine its gas production processes and has long been considered the leader in the field, with a 19 percent global market share.

Through most of the twentieth century, the industrial gas business was an "orderly" market with significant barriers to entry and little direct competition for existing clients or contracts. Capacity was king, and senior managers throughout the industry had a land-grab mind-set: Build plants and pipeline capacity preemptively to dominate local markets, and market share and financial success will follow. In many cases, growth strategy simply amounted to picking a spot on the map, building a plant there, and reasonably expecting to run it at full capacity within three years.

By the late 1980s and early '90s, however, the old order was crumbling as new regional players entered the market and end-user industries such as steel went into decline. When recession hit in the early 1990s, the once orderly market degenerated into a price war for customers. As there was little to differentiate one gas supplier from another, customers did not hesitate to switch to the lowest bidder. The frantic battle for new business led several firms, trapped in their capacity-driven mind-sets, to make ill-considered additions to capacity, with a corresponding deterioration in operating margins for all.

The problem was compounded by Air Liquide's cumbersome, centralized hierarchy, which made many customers feel "abandoned" and "lost." Customers found it took forever to get even basic business information from the company. Simple billing queries frequently developed into complex disputes because of the lack of information and autonomy in local offices. Traditionally, all billing was done from company headquarters on the Quai d'Orsay in Paris, where a huge basement computer cranked out thirty thousand bills a day. Far-flung Air Liquide sales, marketing, and customer service teams were unable to directly access the information and verify the details for their local customers and had to go through multiple layers of the hierarchy to get any information themselves.

No wonder many of the twenty-eight thousand employees of Air Liquide jokingly referred to the company as "The Ministry of Gas."

Air Liquide was caught squarely in the downdraft caused by the shifting marketplace. From the mid-1980s to the early '90s, Air Liquide's three-year rolling average revenue growth dropped from 10 to 2 percent, and operating income growth fell from 10 to −1 percent. The future appeared to be one of stagnant growth, compressed margins, fierce price competition, and increasing commoditization of its products.

A Wake-Up Call from the Customers

Faced with such trends, most materials suppliers reflexively redouble their research and development efforts in search of more efficient production processes and new tweaks to their products. That's what Air Liquide did. It nearly doubled R&D spending to about 3 percent of total revenues.

But when Air Liquide conducted its first customer survey in 1989, it received a shock. Asked to rate the extensive R&D efforts on which the company prided itself, customers overwhelmingly dismissed them as irrelevant. "Customers would have had the same perception of us had we done no R&D at all," says Jean-Renaud Brugerolle, vice president of marketing.

From a customer perspective, this was understandable. Air Liquide's R&D efforts were conducted in a centralized organization, with little input from or interaction with customers. Much of the focus was on creating process improvements for Air Liquide's own operations rather than new offerings for customers, and the product innovations that were developed were often not practical because they were created without an understanding of customers' real needs and business context.

For example, the pulp and paper industry traditionally uses bleach to whiten its products, an environmentally unfriendly practice subject to increasing criticism by eco-activists. Air Liquide discovered an alternative process that used ozone to bleach the paper-pulp. However, the company's innovation

went nowhere for many years because it required re-
designing entire paper mills, a prohibitively expensive
proposition.

Air Liquide's armies of engineers, scientists, and
technically trained managers were chagrined by the
survey results. Clearly, the company and its customers were not on the same page. Simply continuing to invent new products and applications in a
remote R&D laboratory without applying that
know-how more directly to customer needs would
not help Air Liquide preserve its industry dominance
or overcome its growth crisis.

Finding the Hidden Value in Technical Know-How

Air Liquide's traditional technological prowess had
failed to create growth for the company and new
value for customers when applied to traditional
product development, but managers soon learned
that the skills and innovations Air Liquide had developed through its history were a powerful hidden
asset that could be leveraged to create growth if used
in the right way.

The first seed for this new-growth opportunity
came somewhat serendipitously from a new gas production method Air Liquide had been developing to
enable gas production in smaller plants located at the
customer's own factory rather than in central production facilities. Air Liquide was not the first com-

pany to develop on-site production of gases. But after teaming with DuPont to manufacture the membranes widely used in on-site plants, Air Liquide quickly became a leader in the field.

On-site production opened the door to high levels of ongoing interaction between customers and Air Liquide staff and firsthand exposure to customers' business operations. Air Liquide's on-site teams soon discovered that their industrial customers had a variety of pressing needs that they might be able to address, such as improving operating efficiency, increasing the quality of output, and reducing the capital requirements of different processes. After a company reorganization gave greater autonomy to local teams, on-site staff were handed the authority to act on these new opportunities to help customers.

In the process, Air Liquide began to discover that its technical knowledge, which so far had failed to directly produce meaningful product differentiation, could be highly relevant to improving customers' industrial processes. In particular, the know-how and expertise it had developed to run its own plants safely and efficiently could be used to solve customer needs as well. And because Air Liquide had already spent years developing this expertise and field-testing it in its own facilities, the company had no need to go to the considerable expense of creating it from scratch. Customers could be assured that Air Liquide's solutions were robust and could be relied upon to handle mission-critical production activities.

Opening the Magic Chest

What technical know-how did Air Liquide possess that might be valuable to customers? Start with energy efficiency. Just like the industries of many of Air Liquide's customers, gas production is very energy-intensive. In fact, energy accounts for 60 to 65 percent of total gas production costs. Consequently, the company had focused on developing techniques to optimize energy use throughout production, which now could also be applied to the operations of many customers.

Another issue that Air Liquide had in common with its customers was the importance of effectively managing hazardous materials. Simple, seemingly low-risk gases such as oxygen can produce serious fire hazards when concentrated; other gases, harmless by themselves, become toxic when allowed to mix. To manage these issues and comply with increasingly strict regulations, Air Liquide had developed sophisticated measurement and detection systems, quality-control technologies, process automation, pollutant treatment methods, and production planning techniques. Many of these tools and practices had direct applications for customers' hazardous materials processes.

Finally, Air Liquide knew how to distribute gas efficiently to its industrial customers via pipelines, in liquid form via trucks, or in smaller quantities in cylinders. To ensure safety and purity en route, the company had developed a set of tracking and monitoring tools, quality tests, and security measures, all managed from central logistics units. These skills would prove useful in helping customers improve the efficiency of their supply chain and logistics operations.

Air Liquide had a tendency to take these skills and areas of expertise for granted. However, now that the company's on-site teams were developing fresh insights into their customers' needs and economics, they realized that these processes and know-how were more sophisticated than what most of their customers were doing on their own. Tools that had once been considered just a cost of doing business could now become important sources of new revenue and profit.

Manage My Processes for Me, Please

Air Liquide's first efforts to take advantage of its rediscovered expertise centered on integrating new services with its traditional industrial gas products to address these materials handling issues. This allowed the company to differentiate its otherwise commodity products while also earning new service fees. Consider how Air Liquide teamed with BASF, the large German chemicals and plastics manufacturer, to manage all of BASF's gas production and handling activities. BASF had to monitor and manage flows of nitrogen, oxygen, hydrogen, carbon monoxide, and steam from their original sources to the point where they were used in plastics production. This was complicated and costly.

Air Liquide offered to provide BASF with on-site production and management of all these gas flows right up to the point of use, including inventory monitoring, reordering, and on-site distribution management. The company's technicians also handle a range of other gas-related processes for BASF, including the switching of filters and mixers as dictated by production requirements, equipment maintenance, purchase order processing, security, and emissions control. As a result of this far-ranging relationship, gas management costs have dropped significantly for BASF. For example, Air Liquide's astute inventory management practices alone have trimmed 30 percent from BASF's gas costs.

Air Liquide is now the exclusive supplier of all packaged gases at BASF, helps BASF handle shipments from other suppliers, and captures a share of BASF's overall production management expenditures through additional service fees.

Give Me Peace of Mind

These offerings were just the start of Air Liquide's new-growth renaissance. With permanent staff at client sites to handle on-site gas production and basic gas handling services, it was positioned to take over more and more activities that previously had been managed by the customers themselves, addressing broader and more complex needs in the process. Thus, Air Liquide's expanding installed base of on-site gas production facilities was growing into a second important hidden asset, one that was an important mechanism for amortizing the cost of putting service people on-site and learning about the customers' issues. "To sell service is a question of opportunities," says Benoit Potier, director general of Air Liquide. "We use our on-site factories to create such opportunities."

"The real change," adds former CEO Alain Joly, "was not the technology in itself, but the vision of the services market that could develop alongside the technology by responding to the local needs of clients."

One of the things that Air Liquide managers soon learned was that customers were increasingly concerned with more sophisticated needs such as maximizing factory output, minimizing downtime, and limiting environmental and other hazards. To address these issues, Air Liquide used its real-time monitoring expertise to move from helping customers manage gas as a production *input* to taking responsibility for the *output* of gas-based production processes. In doing so, the company would guarantee the output and take on the production risk its customers faced, while earning new profits for its ability to handle these production processes more efficiently.

A good example comes from the food industry. When a company that makes egg-based foods was looking for a way to quick-freeze omelets, Air Liquide was ready. It developed an integrated package of services that included a programmable gas tunnel to adapt quick-freezing parameters to different types of omelets, an automatic liquid nitrogen delivery system, and a quality-control system that uses sensors and analyzers to detect traces of oil, water, or other impurities during food production. This setup reduced the labor required and, more important, sharply reduced the risk of errors and spoilage. And because Air Liquide was paid only for perfectly produced omelets, it was essentially assuming the production risk (and any monetary gains from improved production efficiency) from its customer.

By using its capabilities in gas monitoring and usage control to solve new problems for its customers, Air Liquide also opened up new value-capture opportunities for itself. Rather than simply billing the customer according to the volume of liquid nitrogen consumed, it was now able to charge for an entire package of systems and technology, for consulting and design expertise, and for risk management and quality guarantees. Air Liquide's margins also improved, since these services are far more valuable to customers than a commodity gas alone.

Expanding the Realm of Opportunity

Air Liquide's success in deploying new services to its traditional gas customers was an important source of growth. However, the success also opened management's eyes to the fact that there could be opportunities to deploy its technical know-how for its customers *beyond* Air Liquide's traditional realm of gas. One of those involved moving from managing gases for customers to managing all of their chemical needs.

Texas Instruments, a major chip maker, initially used Air Liquide as a simple supplier of specialty gases to maintain the ultraclean factory environment, grow silicon dioxide on the wafers at the heart of microprocessor chips, and harden chip surfaces. At the time, Texas Instruments manufactured, conditioned, and packaged its own chemicals for use in chip production. Realizing that there were similarities between industrial gas production and chemical production (such as the need for careful management and handling chemicals and the importance of avoiding any impurities) and looking for ways to divest noncore activities, Texas Instruments approached Air Liquide about taking on a role in managing its Chemical Operations Department as Air Liquide had done for the company's gas activities.

Air Liquide quickly recognized that chemicals management could be a valuable way to expand its relationship not just with Texas Instruments, but also with other semiconductor customers. Air Liquide purchased Texas Instruments' chemical operations department in 1997 and now manufactures and supplies chemicals to Texas Instruments as well as offering a full range of support services. For instance, Air Liquide provides round-the-clock, on-site services to manage, analyze, and operate the network of equipment and software that supplies Texas Instruments' factory with gases and chemicals. The company has also expanded its expertise to offer advanced chemical and gas analyses, helping to troubleshoot processes, design diagnostic experiments, and formulate custom chemistries.

The benefits for Texas Instruments are significant. It consolidated its purchasing, quality-control, and emissions management for both gas and chemicals, and the reliability guarantees that Air Liquide provided gave Texas Instruments' managers peace of mind and greater freedom to concentrate on their core business.

For Air Liquide, the acquisition not only increased the amount of revenue received from Texas Instruments, but also deepened the relationship between the two companies. In addition to the provision of gas, Air Liquide now charges Texas Instruments for the efforts of two hundred on-site employees as well as for a broad array of measurement and quality-control services. And according to Christophe Fontaine, an Air Liquide vice president, the relationship is now so deeply embedded that it would take Texas Instruments a number of years to change suppliers should it ever desire to do so.

Most important, the move gave Air Liquide a foothold in the $16 billion industrial chemicals management market. Based on its experience at Texas Instruments, Air Liquide now offers "Total Gas and Chemical Management" solutions to other semiconductor makers, even those that are not customers of Air Liquide's core gas business. Gas and chemical management services are contracted separately from gas supply and are customized based on client requests. The company even goes so far as to conduct joint field research projects with customers, some of which turn into new services that further enhance the value that Air Liquide offers all its clients.

Air Liquide's integrated services clearly demonstrate the impact that hidden assets can have in delivering new value to customers. Its director of electronic products and services comments, "By using our knowledge and experience such as our large databases detailing repair and maintenance histories, we can help clients reduce downtime and production costs, lower maintenance costs, avoid costly quality problems, and reduce investments in spare parts inventory." All are very tangible benefits indeed.

Air Liquide's pursuit of new ways to take advantage of its expertise hasn't stopped with its integrated gas and chemicals services. It has also used its expertise in the management of hazardous materials within its own operations to conceive a suite of services and information systems for optimizing customers' broader supply chains. This offering involves capturing industrial data to enable customers to compare, anticipate, model, and optimize their production runs; optimize output within a single plant or across plants; and remotely manage fixed equipment inventories.

Air Liquide has also moved into the realm of energy production. Many of its customers operate in energy-intensive industries, consuming large amounts of electricity and steam while also trying to control emissions and waste. Because Air Liquide annually uses electricity roughly equal to the production of two average-sized nuclear power plants, it has developed techniques to optimize its use of energy while producing less pollution. In fact, Air Liquide's energy costs declined by 9 percent in 2001 as a direct result of its innovative energy production and optimization efforts.

Armed with this kind of technical expertise, Air Liquide approached Arcelor, Europe's largest steel producer, about collaborating to co-generate power. In its arrangement with Arcelor, Air Liquide purchases gases that are the natural by-products of Arcelor's steel production and uses them to generate electricity. The company uses the electricity itself to lower its production costs and also sells it to customers and electricity companies.

The Evolving Business Mix

By seizing the new opportunities in services, Air Liquide has expanded its potential market from industrial gas to a number of markets that are each two to three times as large. Services have grown from 7 percent of Air Liquide's revenues in 1991 to 22 percent today and are expected to grow to 30 percent by the end of 2003. This represents annual revenue of some $1.8 billion. And because services have much higher margins than the traditional gas supply business, they contribute an even larger share of profits.

This shift away from a sole reliance on gas sales also helps shield Air Liquide from the economic swings that buffet its competitors, allowing it to increase its average revenue per contract and write longer contracts. As Joly explains, "We have worked to disassociate ourselves from swings in the economy by focusing on services and on long-term contracts with our clients. Today, only 15 to 20 percent of our business is still vulnerable to global economic swings."

Fueled by the success of its service offerings, Air Liquide has achieved impressive financial results over the past several years. From 1996 to 2001, the company posted a 10 percent average annual growth in revenue, a 14 percent growth in operating income, and a 9 percent growth in market value—all in a market suffering through a cyclical downturn. As CEO Joly observed in 1999, "Our shift to services will enable us to make our business less capital-intensive. Our objective is to find the right balance between our core business, which generates regular cash flow and profits, and services that require less capital and more knowledge."

Taking a Page from Air Liquide's Playbook

Do you have opportunities to create new growth and new customer value by leveraging existing technical know-how within your organization? The following questions will help you identify opportunities for following in the footsteps of Air Liquide:

- Air Liquide's success began when it realized that it had accumulated skills and expertise that were relevant to customer problems. What unique forms of technical know-how does your organization possess that could be valuable for your customers?
- For a long time, Air Liquide maintained simple commodity-supplier relationships with its customers. Only after it got closer to its customers and understood their real headaches did the company uncover opportunities to become an economic partner. Are there opportunities for you to work more closely with your customers, even taking over some of their own processes?
- Air Liquide's relationship with Texas Instruments became a model for expanding relationships with other semiconductor clients. Do you have a process to codify special projects for large clients and transform them into services that can be offered to a larger array of customers?

PART THREE

---

*Making Growth Happen
in the Real World*

10

Hidden Liabilities: The Other Side of the Ledger

New Growth Is Hard

The stories of Cardinal, OnStar, and the other demand innovators offer inspiring examples of how to grow in powerful new ways. But for managers trained in the ways of product-centric growth, actually achieving this kind of business growth by meeting next-generation demand is uniquely challenging. What exactly makes this shift so hard?

The answer is written in the invisible balance sheet that every large company carries—a ledger not only of hidden assets but also of *hidden liabilities* that impact the firm's ability to recognize and pursue new-growth opportunities.

We'll explore the implications of this concept in the next three chapters. To begin, let's consider how one real-life manager wrestled with the challenge of new growth within a large and slow-growing firm and what she learned in the process.

The Invisible Balance Sheet

Rachel was a senior manager at a large firm that produces plastics for use by consumer electronics companies—makers of phones, radios, calculators, video games, and the like. The company (let's call it Electronic Plastics, Inc., or EPI for short) had been around since the 1940s; ten years ago it was purchased by a Fortune 100 company (Acme, Inc.). During that decade, EPI's revenues had grown, although at a gradually diminishing rate. When we met Rachel, sales growth was down to just around 4 percent annually and profits were stagnant.

The reason for this disappointing performance wasn't mysterious. EPI was one of several plastics makers that served roughly the same customer base with fundamentally similar products. The resulting price competition had battered EPI's margins. In response, Rachel and a handful of her colleagues had been exploring a possible solution, a way out of the commoditization trap. The idea was to help EPI's best customers develop unique, higher-value plastics products by creating a new market research and design capability.

EPI's leadership had liked the concept and authorized a couple of pilot projects. Two years later, both were abandoned, because neither had generated the expected sales or a single dollar in profits. Frustrated and worried, Rachel wanted to explore the reasons why these efforts had faltered. She sat down over sandwiches and coffee with Gary, a trusted colleague she'd worked with for several years, and started to talk through the situation.

"I'm puzzled, Gary," Rachel began. "It's not as though EPI is lacking in assets. In fact, we bring a lot of strengths to the table. To begin with, nobody is better than EPI at modifying plastics for specific customer needs."

"True," Gary agreed.

"EPI is also great at managing the nitty-gritty of production economics—at trimming pennies from the cost of our products. We've had to be. The purchasing guys we do business with seem to live for nothing except beating us down from thirty-two cents a pound to thirty-one cents."

"Also true," said Gary.

"Then there's our strength in R&D. Ever since the company was founded, we've been famous for our technical know-how, and that's still true today. And our best innovations give our customers new ways of using plastic products that save them money or open up new markets."

"Okay," Gary agreed. "So EPI has definite strengths that it should be able to use to create new growth. How about listing them?" Rachel grabbed a sheet of paper, and she and Gary created the following list:

Hidden Assets of EPI

- Materials processing capabilities
- Cost-efficiency skills
- Advanced technical knowledge
- Applications experience

Rachel put down the pen. "There's just one problem with this list," she said. "It's true that we have hidden assets that should work in our favor in creating new growth. But there are other things about our company that work *against* us."

"That's for sure," said Gary. "The biggest one is the way we're affected by the commodity pricing cycle. The plastics we make aren't unique. If our customers couldn't buy from EPI, they could buy something similar from one of half a dozen competitors without a noticeable loss of quality or performance. So the prices we can charge are determined by cyclical factors—business trends, petroleum prices, things like that."

Rachel nodded. "Exactly. And the pricing cycle drives our decision-making processes. When prices are up, we tend to forget about being consumer-oriented—we just charge as much as the market will bear. And when prices are down, our instinct is to hunker down, lay off workers, and cut spending. Remember the last time we went through that? We cut out most of our training programs and half of our marketing budget. And of course the people we lost were mostly the newest, youngest, and most innovative."

Rachel shook her head. "It's really ironic," she said. "The very capabilities that might help us escape from the commodity pricing cycle are the things that get starved by that cycle!

"Furthermore," she continued, "we think in terms of manufacturing products only—that's all we're used to, and we've never learned any other way of doing business. We're great at R&D into the technical details of how to produce a plastic part, but forget about innovative system design to improve our customers' efficiencies."

Rachel and Gary had uncovered the phenomenon of *hidden liabilities*—generally unrecognized features of a company's mind-set and systems that hamper new-growth efforts. Most companies have a treasure trove of unused hidden assets on the left side of this balance sheet. But those assets are usually offset by a swamp of hidden liabilities on the right side. These hidden liabilities can undermine and devour new-growth initiatives before they get off the ground. They cause managers to misread markets, move too late, execute poorly, underfund initiatives (or drown them in *too much* money), or fail to build commitment to new growth.

Rachel drafted a second list, representing the other side of her company's invisible ledger:

Hidden Liabilities of EPI

- Mind-set molded by commodity pricing cycle
- Manufacturing culture and tradition
- Flawed budgeting process
- No service experience or capability
- No design capability

"All right," Gary said. "So we have an idea about the strengths and weaknesses that EPI brings to the table. Do you think EPI's pilot new-growth projects might have succeeded if not for the hidden liabilities on this list?"

After a moment, Rachel replied, "Not necessarily. There's another liability I hadn't thought about before." At the bottom of the list, she added:

• Lack of customer readiness

"I'm not sure I understand that one," Gary said.

"Here's what I mean," Rachel responded. "In our pilot programs, we tried to develop some innovative ideas for plastics that could help our customers create new-product designs that end users would really love. But only about a third of our customers were even interested in talking about the idea with us. Finding a customer willing to really partner with us was really hard."

"Hmm. Maybe that means the idea didn't really match up with a customer need."

Rachel shook her head. "No, it wasn't that. The problem wasn't the idea. It was the people we were talking to—our customer contacts. We were working through the same purchasing guys we'd always done business with. Innovative design just isn't their thing. We needed to connect with a higher level of management at our customers' firms . . . but we never did."

"I wonder what it would take for us to do that," Gary said.

Rachel thought for a long moment. Then a lightbulb lit. "EPI may not have any way to make those connections . . . but Acme does. They've got a

bunch of service businesses that are deeply entrenched at some of our customers' companies. I bet
we could get to their senior managers through
Acme's senior managers . . . and to their design and
product development departments through Acme's
marketing division." She grabbed the Hidden Assets
list and scrawled a new item at the bottom:

• Customer access through Acme

The exercise of listing and studying the relationship between EPI's hidden assets and its hidden liabilities had helped clarify for Rachel why the firm's
previous efforts to create new growth had failed, and
it had identified a previously unexplored asset that
might make a difference the next time.

Stepping-Stones and Roadblocks

Rachel's story is not unique. Given half a chance,
most managers can identify the barriers to new
growth *even more easily* than they can name the opportunities and hidden assets that can propel their
business forward. They bang their shins against these
obstacles all the time. That's why comments like
these arise almost spontaneously from managers dis-
cussing their businesses:

- "We make bold statements about growth. But when the budget crunch hits, new initiatives are the first things to get cut."
- "We have a lot of good ideas about growth here, but they're mixed in with a lot of *bad* ones. So the senior managers tend to throw up their hands and just wait for them all to go away."
- "Integrated customer support? Sounds like a great concept. But it won't work here. Our organizational structure is oriented around separate business units. We spend our time figuring out how to divide our turf and our profits, not working together for the customers."
- "I'd love to launch an initiative based on our information assets. But first I need systems that'll do what they're supposed to do for *today's* business—let alone tomorrow's."

Such laments illustrate the mechanisms by which hidden liabilities interfere with the development of new-growth initiatives in almost all organizations.

In some cases, a particular element of your business can be *both* an asset and a liability. For example, a company's brand is a powerful asset that conveys information about your company's identity and builds customer trust. Yet the same brand can be a liability that inhibits new growth. A company with powerful brand recognition in one area may be so deeply entrenched that it is unable to win its customers' permission to move into a new-growth area. The Xerox brand, for example, was synonymous with copiers. But the company's position in that space did not confer authority to become a corporate "document manager," and Xerox's attempt to expand its business into that marketplace faltered.

The lesson: *Demand innovation requires different raw materials than traditional growth—different skills, different organizational structures, different metrics and compensation, and sometimes a different brand.*

The problem isn't that there is something "wrong" with the people in place (who are bright, hardworking, and well meaning), nor with the systems and structures they manage (which were developed for good reasons pertinent to the core business). But it's unrealistic to expect an old system of thought, accounting, metrics, and management to produce and nurture a new system on its own. That's why hidden liabilities must be consciously identified, studied, understood, and overcome or managed as part of your request for new growth.

Types of Hidden Liabilities

The list of hidden liabilities is open-ended; you can probably suggest variations peculiar to your own company. But here are the basic types of hidden liabilities we've identified:

The Dirty Dozen: Hidden Liabilities

Cultural Liabilities

- Corporate mind-set
- Culture and history
- Leadership and commitment

Structural Liabilities

- Organizational structure
- Skills and capabilities
- Measurements and incentive systems
- Budgeting and resource allocation processes
- Information systems

External Liabilities

- Brand/authority
- Customer readiness
- Investor resistance
- Distribution channels/alliances

One liability is usually enough to hamper a growth move; two or three acting together are usually fatal. Every business has an assortment of them. They must be identified, mapped, and even quantified so that the executives who want to create new growth will know how to navigate around them.

Let's consider some of these hidden liabilities and the problems they can cause.

Antibodies Run Amok: Cultural Liabilities

If you work at a large established firm, the chances are good that your corporate culture has been successful, honed through years or even decades of product-driven growth. But when growth has slowed or stopped, the very momentum that kept the ship on course becomes dangerous. The same system of management controls that helps focus team members on the key factors that drive the core business limits their ability to understand and try new approaches.

A familiar example is the type of risk aversion that characterizes most large firms. This begins as a natural and necessary defense mechanism. Every company must define itself, and this includes defining what it is *not*—the kinds of business it will stay away from as well as those it will pursue. The act of self-definition generates institutional "antibodies" that guard the margins of the corporation. In time, managers learn to rely on these antibodies to protect them from funding poorly conceived ventures: the new product based on a request from a single customer, the solution that addresses last year's problem, or the hasty e-business initiative. Organizations survive in part because they can reject wasteful ideas.

But sometimes the antibodies run amok. Rather than protecting the core business, they actually weaken it by attacking any symptom of change.

The signs of this debilitating condition vary. For instance, some corporate cultures avoid growth through the continual retelling of a killer anecdote—a tale of failed innovation that supposedly proves the folly of trying to change. Since most big companies have tried almost everything at least once, there's always an anecdote available for this purpose.

Other companies devote inordinate amounts of time, energy, and intelligence to studying and then arguing about new-growth ideas. A manager at one of the biggest equipment manufacturers sardonically describes his company as "the greatest debating society in the world." He explains: "When someone proposes a new-business concept, we're sure to spend our time talking about the one customer it *won't* work for . . . and forget about the ninety-nine that it *might* work for. In the end, we wear people down with a stream of 'yeah, buts' that focus only on the negatives, never on how we could overcome those negatives."

In cases like these, it's clear that the antibodies are out of control. But the function of corporate self-definition that the antibodies originally served remains an important one. It would be foolish to expect a steel manufacturer to learn to create brilliant advertising . . . to expect bankers to design jet aircraft . . . to expect a carmaker to publish best-selling books . . . or to expect a fast-food company to excel at timber harvesting. These changes are simply too great a stretch to be realistic.

But most companies don't need to make a huge stretch like the weird examples we've just listed.

Most just need to expand their capabilities into new but neighboring areas that will enable them to broaden their offerings while maintaining and strengthening their core businesses. Unfortunately, too many companies have fine-tuned their business systems to the point that virtually *any* stretch into new offerings, no matter how natural and evolutionary, feels impossible.

By all means, think hard about your organization's self-definition. Don't lose your edge and your focus by making that definition overly broad. But don't make the opposite error of allowing your self-definition to become so rigid that it is incapable of evolving over time. When you do this, it changes from an asset into a liability.

Another growth dysfunction occurs when companies give lip service to the notion of growth without actually taking the steps needed to pursue it.

One symptom is a mismatch between senior executives' stated priorities and the way they spend the bulk of their time, energy, and political capital. Many CEOs who say that they are focused on customers and on growing the business actually spend the bulk of their time on such activities as investor relations, operational reviews, succession planning, and organizational coaching. When it comes to growth, they are missing in action. They may announce new-growth initiatives with fanfare, but they fail to follow up with serious funding, high-quality staffing, and the kind of detailed *personal* attention that signals real commitment.

The problem is compounded by widespread passivity among directors. If board members provide no serious, sustained, and informed pressure for new growth, there will be no sense of urgency proportionate to the magnitude of the challenge.

Board members need to develop two new habits. One is continually asking, "Where is this company's next-generation growth coming from?" and insisting on substantive answers. The other is persistently following up on new-growth ideas rather than letting them drop off the radar. These forms of positive pressure can play a big role in keeping the CEO and other managers focused on growth rather than being distracted by fire fighting or settling for programs of old-profit maintenance.

The current mood of renewed involvement and activism among board members may be a healthy sign of change—so long as directors do not learn the *wrong* lessons from the dot-com meltdown and the market traumas of 2001–2002. The problem of stagnation won't be solved by timidly drawing back from business innovation, but rather by focusing intelligently on the *real* sources of new growth in the decade to come.

Burdens of Proof: Structural Liabilities

A company's reluctance to recognize the need for new growth or to take the necessary steps to pursue it is often expressed in the formal structures the company creates to manage its operations.

In many firms, organizational bureaucracies impose an onerous decision cycle on new-growth initiatives. Ideas travel up and down several layers of management in a months-long consensus-building ritual. Meanwhile, the marketplace is moving faster than the ideas can move through the corporate strata. In the end, the ideas get watered down, disappear, or simply become irrelevant. This form of review is often called *due diligence;* it really amounts to *death by a thousand cuts.*

Budgeting systems are among the most effective structural methods for killing new growth. At many large enterprises, the budget process assumes that any new-growth initiative is riskier than any traditional investment. That's true even if the company has had bad experiences with traditional investments, such as building an unprofitable overseas plant, launching a marginally relevant new product, or spending hundreds of millions on R&D with minimal payback

As a result, there are inconsistent standards for allocating investment money. For the core business, winning approval is difficult. For a new-growth idea, it's virtually impossible.

Further hampering new-growth initiatives is the fixed-plant mind-set, which treats every investment as if it were a sunk-cost manufacturing facility, an all-or-nothing upfront investment with a ten-year breakeven horizon. This is exacerbated by an emphasis on preserving current margin at all costs, as well as the popularity of so-called economic-value-added analysis (EVA). As a result, many businesses are under pressure to maximize their current return on capital by improving their plant utilization, reducing inventory levels, and so on.

These are worthwhile goals. But viewing an early-stage growth initiative in terms of EVA and margins ensures paralysis. Since the early years of any growth initiative are likely to consume earnings, the refrain becomes, "We can't afford to grow." New sets of metrics that focus on *total incremental profits* and *long-term return on capital* must be used to measure the potential of today's new-growth moves.

The fact is that next-generation growth opportunities are often materially different from the core business in terms of their underlying economics, capital structure, and methods of capturing value. They have different needs and different requirements for success, and they need to be assessed and organized accordingly.

Creating new growth also calls for different kinds of staff talent than the core business. Consider, for example, the challenges faced by manufacturers when they move toward providing services to improve the customers' economics.

Traditional manufacturing strategy has been built on three foundations: vertical integration of supply and production activities; disciplined research and development to create superior products; and market dominance to provide economies of scale. Naturally, the managers who rise within manufacturing companies are those who excel at these skills. But these aren't the skills needed to guide a service-oriented new-growth initiative or to build new senior-level customer partnerships. When such an initiative is launched, it's headed by either a top-flight manager with fine manufacturing skills poorly matched to the assignment, or (more often) a second-rate manager with mediocre manufacturing skills for whom a "harmless" slot is created. Neither approach is likely to work.

To achieve success in a new-business arena, companies must acquire the new talents needed. But one difficulty in acquiring new talent is that managers (naturally) prefer to hire people who are like themselves. Hence the tendency for companies to self-replicate rather than evolve their skill mix over time.

To solve this problem of talent inertia, companies will need to invest more time, money, and energy to learn how to hire and manage new types of employees with the skills needed to run the new-growth business. Strive to keep the failures to a minimum, by all means; but expect some failures, and use them to succeed the next time.

Finally, most established companies have measurement, management, and information systems that are poorly designed or too inflexible to support the demands of new growth. Finely tuned to the needs of the existing business, they are rarely flexible enough to shift seamlessly to the kinds of operations that further new growth.

Some of these systems problems are so extreme that they are funny . . . unless you are one of the managers thwarted by them. A man we'll call Tom wanted to find new-growth avenues for the auto materials company he worked for, which was a division of a much larger enterprise. Tom spent countless hours with his contacts at the carmakers studying how they used the fabrics his firm made and coming up with ideas about the new services Tom's company could provide.

Finally, all Tom's work seemed ready to pay off. His company was offered a two-year, $12 million contract by one of the Big Three automakers to develop a new program for environmentally sound production and disposal of car parts. Imagine Tom's chagrin when he learned that his company's accounting systems *could not accept* the $12 million in new revenues. The computers were programmed to recognize and record income *only* when it was measured in terms of yards of fabric sold!

Tom spent the next three months wrangling with his company's accounts receivable department . . . rather than negotiating similar lucrative deals with other carmakers.

You might assume that only an old-school manufacturing firm could possibly be so myopic. But in 1993, the same thing happened to one of the world's biggest software makers when it expanded from selling packaged software to selling systems, services, and consulting. Could it happen at your company? Test a new-growth move and see.

Given the prevalence of these kinds of structural liabilities, no wonder many executives simply stop their internal new-growth efforts. They'd rather build another factory (and hope to book enough business to keep it running) or overpay to acquire an existing business than endure the painful process of seriously evaluating new-growth proposals, pushing the best ideas through a torturous decision-making process, and then struggling to make changes in IT systems and other structures they've struggled for years to create, debug, and unify.

This is a bad mistake. Overcoming the structural liabilities you face is a tough challenge, but it can be done. And your chances of attaining double-digit earnings growth *without* taking on that challenge are very small.

Permission to Grow: External Liabilities

Even beyond the internal liabilities that must be overcome to achieve new growth, there are a number of external liabilities you can expect to face—functions of relationships with outside entities that may hamper any attempts to grow.

As we've seen, the brand—often a significant hidden asset—may also be an external liability. This can happen when the brand is difficult or impossible to extend into a natural new-growth space, as with the earlier example of Xerox.

Allied to the issue of brand is that of customer readiness—the willingness of customers to grant a company the authority to extend its reach into a new business arena. Remember Rachel from EPI. One of the obstacles her company faced when trying to expand into new business areas was the resistance of customers, most of whom remained focused on lopping a penny or two off the price per pound rather than on how EPI could create new forms of value for them.

Channel conflict is another form of external liability, one that's painfully familiar to most suppliers. (If you want to see a manufacturer wince in pain, just ask, "So how's it going with the dealers?") Many traditional supplier–distributor relationships are like bad marriages. Each party knows by heart the other's flaws and overlooks the good traits. Each nurses "if-only" dreams about how perfect life would be without the other. Hence, the incredible lure of the myth of disintermediation: "If only we could use digital technology to sell direct and get rid of those middlemen!"

Channel conflict has helped to kill many new-growth initiatives. Ford tried to do an end run around its dealer network in 1998 by launching a website where customers could comparison-shop among a national selection of used and off-lease Ford cars. Amid howls of protest from the dealers, the Texas Motor Vehicle Division took Ford to court on the grounds that it was breaking a law prohibiting automakers from selling directly to the public. Ford lost the case and had to abandon its website in a humiliating retreat.

Similarly, toy retailers helped derail Mattel's Barbie Online program, and value-added computer distributors have blocked efforts by PC makers to emulate the high-efficiency, build-to-order direct sales model pioneered by Dell.

A similar liability emerges with external alliances.

Many companies find that alliances they entered into years ago for reasons that were valid at the time are now barriers to new initiatives. Can Dell Computer pursue any new-growth initiative that would alienate Microsoft or Intel? Can McDonald's pursue new-growth moves that would anger Coca-Cola or Disney? Or vice versa?

Finally, a company's investors may be a significant growth liability. CEOs and other top executives spend hours every month talking with analysts from mutual fund and brokerage firms. Their purpose is to sell the company's strategy to investors and convince them that financial performance is on track. It's a crucial part of the capitalist system. Yet the resulting burden of investor expectations can constrain corporate activity. It's scary to deviate from the point of view that's shared by most analysts who follow an industry, and selling them on a new approach can be very difficult. Unresponsive investors may resist new business ideas or necessary shifts in strategic direction.

In other instances, a company's history and its position within the equities market may constrain it. For example, a company whose stock has long been considered suitable for widows and orphans (in itself a perfectly valid investor segmentation) dare not sacrifice current earnings or cut dividends to fund growth initiatives. Just as the brand may need to evolve in order to earn permission from customers to create a new kind of business, the image of a stock may need to evolve in order to retain the favor of investors even as the profit model changes.

The Message of the Invisible Balance Sheet

Any company that hopes to leverage its hidden assets to create new growth must candidly identify and assess its hidden liabilities, then systematically look for ways to neutralize, minimize, or work around them. Start the way Rachel did, by listing both the hidden assets and the hidden liabilities of your company. Then evolve both lists over time.

This exercise serves two purposes. One is to reveal the hidden rocks on which your growth moves will founder unless you navigate around them. The second is to clarify the nature of the system that has been built up in your company and the degree to which it might impede new growth.

Then ask these questions:

- What are the most important hidden liabilities that prevent you from creating new growth?
- Has your organization ever overcome any of these liabilities in the past? If so, how? If not, have other organizations overcome similar liabilities? If so, how?
- In what ways can your liabilities be neutralized, minimized, or circumvented?
- Who are the people, both inside and outside your organization, who can act to do so? What exactly do they need to do?

- What kinds of acquisitions, alliances, or other business design moves might help you overcome your hidden liabilities?

A burst of heroics by an inspired CEO or other executive may lead the occasional growth initiative to victory through sheer force of intellect or personality. But heroics alone cannot build a growth *system*. That requires identifying the particular hidden liabilities, then focusing relentlessly on overcoming them.

In the next two chapters, we'll examine two key steps in building an operating system for growth. The first is freeing the creative powers of the middle managers—a cadre of potential leaders who know their company's hidden assets and hidden liabilities better than anyone, and who will help catalyze change if encouraged (or simply permitted) to do so. The second is making a series of key adjustments in an organization's decision-making, resource-deployment, and goal-setting systems.

Much of the energy your company needs to make new growth happen is already in place. Now you need to learn how to mobilize it.

11

The Role of the Middle Manager: Becoming a Growth Catalyst

Growth Is Your *Problem*

If you're a middle manager in a no-growth company, you may feel that much of the excitement of work has been drained away. Prospects for promotions and raises are dim. The value of stock options is stagnant or even shrinking. Perhaps worst of all, you have few chances to use your energies and talents creatively. Boxed in by your company's hidden liabilities, you spend too much time fighting defensive actions and not enough time pursuing new markets and new-growth opportunities.

In the previous chapter, we introduced you to two middle managers: Rachel of EPI, who was struggling to help her firm break out of its commoditization trap, and Tom, whose company systems simply couldn't handle the innovative $12 million contract he'd developed.

Here's a sobering truth: The two real-life managers behind these disguised portraits both quit their no-growth firms within three years of the incidents we described.

Unfortunately, there's never any guarantee that the grass on the other side of the fence is really as green as it appears. Those who migrated to Silicon Valley and the dot-coms during the late 1990s in search of high-growth pastures can attest to that.

If you're one of the many middle managers at established firms, the growth crisis is today's biggest problem. And it is, in the truest sense, *your* problem, not the problem of the CEO or the senior managers. In many companies, the top leaders will retire sometime in the next five years. (Why not? The business is tougher now than ever.) And since any substantive new-growth initiatives they launch won't pay off for longer than five years, their motivation to act is quite low.

For middle managers, the picture is quite different. You won't be retiring for another fifteen or twenty years—the dwindling value of 401(k) plans has made that likely. So *your* decisions will shape the future of your company; the actions you choose to take over the next five years will determine the company's stock price ten years from now.

Leaving your no-growth firm may be an option to consider, but it's not the only option. As this chapter will show, middle managers are far from helpless. You can play a powerful role in leveraging your companies' hidden assets, overcoming hidden liabilities, and creating new-growth opportunities.

What follows is a story about a real-life middle manager who is playing this catalytic role in her company. By reaching out beyond her formal sphere of control and creatively surmounting barriers, she is making growth happen despite her company's growth-unfriendly culture.

The Middle Manager Makes the Difference

Kathy is a vice president at a big company we'll call Magnum Manufacturing. We visited her recently to learn the story behind Magnum's successful launch of an innovative service business—Kathy's brain-child—which promises to be a source of new growth for at least the next decade and probably longer. What we heard was a classic tale of how a middle manager can expand her own growth opportunities as well as those of her company by being inventive, opportunistic, dogged, and a little subversive.

"I've been with Magnum for fourteen years," Kathy began, "so I thought I knew all about the difficulties of trying to start anything new here. But I have to tell you, it's been even harder than I expected.

"It's not that people here don't recognize the need for growth. Believe me, they get that. Between 1997 and 2000, our product sales were flat, and we had to lay off 20 percent of our people just to stay profitable. We closed three offices and stopped handing out promotions. It was depressing.

"But in 1999, I started thinking about some new ideas for extending our business by creating a new integrated service offering for our customers. The more I studied the possibilities and discussed them with experts in the field and some of our younger managers, the more excited I got. It looked like this was a real growth opportunity.

"I went to Jerry with the concept. He's the president of our division and the guy who would have to approve the new venture. But he couldn't see the idea at first. In fact, he had a lot of objections: 'We don't know how to build a service business. We don't have a service staff or the sales force we would need to sell our services. And we don't even understand the finances of a service business. All we know is manufacturing.'

"Frankly, everything Jerry said was valid. But I knew the idea had merit, and I kept after him. 'We don't need to start with a big investment,' I said. 'Let's give it a try on a small scale and expand the business later if it works.' Jerry turned me down, not once but half a dozen times. I nagged and cajoled, but I couldn't break through his reluctance to shift any focus from our core business."

So Kathy's attempts to launch her new-growth idea by following the processes laid down in the corporate manual went nowhere. Fortunately, she was too stubborn and too firmly convinced of the value of her idea to let the matter drop. How did she finally get the level of approval she needed to move forward?

"It took quite a while. But about a year after I first proposed the new business, Jerry was getting just a little desperate. We'd had another down year. The stock was going nowhere. Headquarters was sending signals that we'd better find a way to grow or else. Jerry started listening to me a little harder.

"Finally, after I'd assembled a mass of analysis to back up the service concept and presented them in the boardroom to Jerry and the key members of his team, I decided it was time to give it a hard push. I turned to an outside consultant we'd hired—a very knowledgeable and respected guy—and I asked him in front of Jerry and the whole team, 'What would General Electric do with an opportunity like this?'

"The consultant said, 'They would launch some pilots—and they would do it *now.*'

"With that public prodding, Jerry finally relented. Six months later, we had pilot projects running in two markets."

We were impressed with the persistence and effectiveness of Kathy's lobbying efforts, which ultimately opened a door that had appeared to be permanently locked. But we wondered where she'd found the resources to research and develop her idea while courting her boss's approval.

She laughed. "I didn't really *have* any resources, at least none worth talking about. I wasn't sitting at a desk on the executive floor mapping out strategy on a legal pad. I was making things happen personally, kind of like the spark plug in an engine. And the work was just about as gritty and greasy as that makes it sound.

"Getting people's time and energy for this project was all done on a begged-and-borrowed basis. We had a young woman in our accounting department who was brilliant and bored—in fact, she was ready to leave the company. I convinced her boss to assign her to me for six months. He was happy to get her off his back—to him, Diane was simply a problem. It turned out that she was a fantastic manager. She helped pull together the service business idea and is now director of operations for the new division—her third promotion in two years.

"Then there was Tony. He used to run our Canadian operation, which folded after losing money for three years. It wasn't Tony's fault, but internally he took the blame for it. In the normal course of events, Tony would have hung on until retirement, not doing much and certainly not rising in the corporation. Instead, I asked to have him assigned to our new project. His deal-making talent, which no one had really recognized, suddenly came to the fore. He got involved in crafting all the partnerships we needed to set up the service business, and now he's our director of alliances.

"Diane and Tony both shone when they were given a chance to work on something new—an opportunity no one in Magnum had had in years. And they put in plenty of fifteen-hour days along with me to make it happen, believe me."

Two lessons from Kathy's story were emerging. First, Kathy would never have built her new initiative if she'd waited for the ideal corporate support to get started. Instead, she developed the idea, championed it tirelessly, and made it easy for her boss to commit by focusing early on a few simple pilots.

Second, Kathy developed the resources she needed largely by finding people whose talents were underused and liberating them—giving a human face to the concept of hidden assets. But we wondered whether three people were enough to create a new business.

"No, we needed a lot more help. So the three of us talked up our project around the company and got other people to contribute a little time and effort— off the sides of their desks, so to speak. We'd have a person in production doing some research, a couple of people from finance crunching some numbers, a guy in marketing coming up with some ideas. We invited smart people from various divisions to participate in brainstorming sessions . . . that kind of thing.

"It worked because people got excited about the idea of trying something new that made business sense for our company. Plus we didn't make a lot of demands on them. And we had food at the meetings. That's one of the big lessons I learned: Serve food and people will show up." Kathy laughed again. (You may have noticed that Kathy tends to laugh a lot. A sense of humor may be one of the prerequisites for pulling off a success like hers.)

It seemed clear that Magnum's culture and systems had created roadblocks for Kathy's new-growth initiative, forcing her to use the improvisational tactics she described. We asked Kathy whether being part of Magnum had done anything to *help* her in creating the new business.

"Are you kidding? Magnum's assets played a *big* role. Being part of Magnum means people at other companies return our phone calls. And when we offer to create an alliance, they sometimes agree partly because of who we are. They like to tell their clients, 'Oh, we have a new alliance with Magnum, you know.'

"And some of Magnum's distributors have bought into our concept and have created markets for us. One distributor in Florida got us $60,000 worth of business the first month. That opened a few eyes around headquarters to the potential of the business.

"Of course, making the most of our position sometimes meant skirting traditional corporate guidelines. The key competency for the service business we were creating was being able to make deals, even difficult or implausible ones. This isn't something that the rules and systems at Magnum encourage. But we discovered that Tony is brilliant at finding ways to work things out, even if it takes improvising around standard procedures or corporate policies. So we set him loose and let him work his magic.

"All in all, it's tricky—figuring out how to use the hidden assets of Magnum without being dragged down by the hidden liabilities. The guys in corporate purchasing sometimes call and want us to let them set up our partnerships the same way they buy parts for the manufacturing business—using standardized deal memos. We have to fight them off. Ours is a different business that has to be run separately. We politely stall them, 'lose' their memos, and eventually they back down . . . only to start all over again every time someone new is put in charge of purchasing.

"Same with our advertising. At first, we worked with the big multinational agency that handles Magnum's corporate account. To them we were small potatoes; they did nothing for us. Now we've gotten autonomy and linked up with a little partnership to do our marketing communications. We behave like entrepreneurs, even though we're part of Magnum." She smiled. "I have to admit, it's kind of fun."

We asked Kathy, "So what was the *toughest* thing about launching a new-growth initiative inside a new-growth incumbent?"

Kathy rolled her eyes. "It sounds petty, but the toughest thing is that I got so little encouragement. There was never a 'Nice job, Kathy' from my boss. Three words like that would be the equivalent of winning the Nobel Peace Prize." She sighed. "But that's Jerry's personality—he's an engineer—and even more, it's the culture around here. In most parts of Magnum, I mean," she corrected herself. "I think it's a little different in *my* department."

Today, Kathy's start-up is operational in thirty-eight states, with six more in the planning stages. It's not the largest business unit in Jerry's operation—yet—but it's the fastest-growing one. And many of the smartest and most energetic young people from around the corporation have been sending their résumés to Kathy . . . "just in case you have an opening anytime soon."

Expanding Your Zone of Control

It's the nature of middle management to own a *limited zone of control* . . . a neat little box on an organizational chart that supposedly defines what you can and cannot do. Some of the frustrations of being a middle manager grow directly out of this limitation.

It's true that you're not the CEO. You have people you must answer to. Of course, so does the CEO. There are genuine limits to what you can do without help from the system in which you work. But as Kathy's story vividly illustrates, the space you control is much larger than you may think.

The reason is that the nature of the corporate box within which you manage is quite different from what it appears. On the organizational chart, the boundaries of the box appear static and fixed. The lines of command, control, and communication that connect your box with other boxes appear clear and unchangeable, and the empty spaces that separate the boxes appear pristine and inviolable.

But experience teaches that all these appearances are illusions. The boundaries of the box are not fixed but flexible. The lines that connect the boxes can be multiplied and redrawn, and the empty spaces that separate the boxes can be bridged.

Think about how Kathy expanded the boundaries of her space. She did it by salvaging Diane and Tony from the business scrap heap and setting them loose on an exciting new-business idea . . . by using her own enthusiasm to attract energies from elsewhere in the company . . . by lobbying her boss with persistence, imagination, and good humor until he finally flashed a reluctant green light . . . by ignoring some of the operational strictures imposed by other corporate boxes . . . and even by serving turkey sandwiches at her brainstorming sessions.

The lessons of Kathy's story become apparent only through action. The more you act on the factors you can control, the more the boundaries of your box will seem to recede. It's not about getting outside your box or erasing its walls. It's about expanding the box. The box is organic. Its boundaries can be stretched, provided you refuse to be ruled by negative assumptions . . . and provided you aren't too picky about the methods you use.

Following Kathy's Path: Opportunities for Middle Managers

Overcoming the obstacles that are typically found at large firms isn't easy—but it can be done. Once you choose to grow the box in which you operate, the special opportunities you enjoy as a middle manager will begin to become apparent.

As a middle manager, you have a hands-on understanding of your company's invisible balance sheet. The hidden assets and liabilities of an organization are often most apparent from a ground-level view.

Only the information manager who actually works every day with a particular database really understands the wealth of customer data it contains . . . and can ask how it could be used to tailor offerings more precisely to individual end users.

Only the manager who accompanies sales reps on calls to the company's biggest customers really knows about the quirks in the ordering system that drive clients crazy . . . and has an idea about how to create a new ordering system that would not only repair the glitches but also provide improved service that customers would be willing to pay for.

Only the production manager who personally adjusts manufacturing schedules really knows which customers most often require rush deliveries and of which products . . . and can suggest a system for capturing that added value through variable pricing.

Think about the unique position you occupy in your corporation. What insights into your company's hidden assets and liabilities does it yield? How can these be used as the basis for a possible new-growth idea? Then feel your corporate box beginning to expand.

As a middle manager, you've already helped solve customer problems. These days, most top executives from the CEO on down have learned to talk the customer talk. But let's face it—as a middle manager, you touch customer concerns far more often than the typical CEO, probably on a daily basis. You are the person to whom complaints from the end users, the sales force, and the distribution channels are directed; you hear immediately about how the products work (and don't work) and what people say about your pricing, packaging, advertising, marketing, and service.

As a result, chances are good that you have seen or helped create one or more small-scale innovations to serve your customers better. They may be simple things—for example, tracking the product assembly data that customers ask about most often and gathering it in a binder with tabs for easy reference by the folks who answer your phones. But an innovation like this may contain the seeds of a new-growth initiative.

Ask yourself: *How can my best customer-focused idea be turned into a profit center and expanded?* Then go ahead and do it. Your corporate box will grow in the process.

As a middle manager, you can operate below the corporate radar. You've seen how the cumbersome decision-making processes at most big companies tends to stymie new-growth moves. Follow Kathy's example: Rather than allowing the system to stop you, work around it. Launch your new-growth idea in the form of a small pilot project that can be run off the side of your desk. Free up a few hours a week from each of your brightest, most frustrated eager beavers and set them loose on it. At every step of the way, gather data to document what you've learned about costs, market potential, customer reactions, and other nitty-gritty exceptional details.

By the time you absolutely *have* to have your boss's okay on a budget line or his signature on a business plan, you may find that your pilot project is already generating revenues, satisfying customers, creating excitement, and winning friends both inside and outside your organization. How can your boss say "No" to something like that? He'll have little choice but to formally ratify the fact that your box has, in fact, already been redefined.

As a middle manager, you are part of the most powerful network in the corporation. When Harry Truman left the presidency, he remarked that his successor, Dwight D. Eisenhower, was in for a bit of a shock. "He'll sit at his desk and give orders," Truman predicted, "and then discover that nothing happens."

Many a rueful CEO has learned Truman's lesson. The truth is that in most organizations nothing happens unless the middle managers want it to happen. They are the people who translate corporate strategy into practical plans; who hire, fire, motivate, train, coach, inspire, and guide front-line employees; and who determine by their actions or inactions whether or not the CEO's latest fiat is meaningful or dead on arrival.

This reality can be frustrating for top executives. But for the middle manager, it should be profoundly empowering. You and your peers have the corporate destiny in your hands, if only you realize your power and choose to wield it.

How can you use your status as part of the middle manager network on behalf of next-generation growth for your company? Here are three ways:

1. **Support the Kathys throughout your organization.** Be on the lookout for smart growth ideas wherever they originate, and lend them your vocal encouragement, your time, and your energy.
2. **Enlist the support of other middle managers for your own growth moves.** As Kathy did, get

the word out about the new initiatives you are launching, and don't be shy about asking other departments to contribute on a manageable scale their unique expertise and capabilities.

3. **Model growth-oriented thinking and behavior for the rest of the company.** Consciously work to set a positive tone in your interactions up, down, and across the corporate hierarchy. Show by your example how both individuals and the organization as a whole can learn to stretch their skills in new and profitable directions.

We opened this chapter with a fairly grim picture of the problems facing the middle manager in a no-growth business. That picture was real. We close with an optimistic picture of the enormous opportunities middle managers enjoy. That, too, is real. Which reality the future will resemble is largely up to you.

It would be nice to promise a trouble-free, frictionless future to middle managers who choose to stay and work to bring new growth to the embattled companies. But remember that if you follow this path, your central role must be to serve as a spark plug in the corporate engine—and no spark was ever generated without friction.

So expect resistance, setbacks, failures, mistakes, and uncertainty. But if you follow the middle manager's path with energy and integrity, we can promise that whatever happens, you surely won't be bored. And with a bit of luck, you just *may* find yourself at the leading edge of a new day of corporate renewal.

12

The Job of the Senior Manager: Creating an Operating System for Growth

If you are a CEO, a senior executive, or a board member at an established company, you may be feeling a little uncomfortable now.

In the previous two chapters, we've looked at the dark side of the corporate balance sheet—the hidden liabilities that serve to stifle new-growth opportunities at most companies. We've also highlighted the critical role of inspired middle managers and the internal battles they must win to bring innovative thinking to life.

Perhaps you've found yourself wondering *Is it really that tough to pursue innovation in our company? Have we created an operating system that's unfriendly to new growth?*

Of course, only the people who report to you can answer those questions. And they may or may not be willing to do so . . . depending on the level of trust and openness you've managed to establish. If your company is typical, the picture painted in the last two chapters is realistic.

So what can you do about it?

Most senior managers know intuitively that it's not good enough to rely on the inspired efforts of a few maverick managers (the Kathys of the world) to find and nurture new-growth opportunities. In most companies, the number of talented mavericks can be counted on the fingers of one hand . . . and all too often, they simply leave when the frustration becomes great enough. Putting the whole burden of change on the shoulders of the few mavericks will only lead to further stagnation.

Success in creating new growth again and again requires that your organization develop an operating system to identify, shape, and nurture new-growth initiatives. And the responsibility for developing such an operating system lies with the senior management team and ultimately with the CEO. If you're a member of that team, consider yourself retitled for the duration of this chapter as CGO . . . Chief Growth Officer. Everything we say here will focus on that role.

Of course, achieving that goal isn't easy. Senior managers get hung up on a series of genuinely thorny issues:

- How do you create innovative new-growth initiatives without losing your focus on the core business?
- How do you respond to the pressure for short-

term earnings while funding growth initiatives that may not be immediately profitable?

- How do you support innovative thinkers and risk takers without signaling neglect or abandonment of the core business?
- How do you separate the truly promising growth opportunities from moves that could endanger the company or are likely to produce only marginal improvements?

The tensions reflected in these questions are real. Managing along these fault lines is a long-term discipline rather than a problem to be solved once and for all, and no single set of formulas will fit all companies. The growth equation that works for Cardinal Health isn't the same as the one developed by Johnson Controls.

However, examining the practices of these firms and others that have achieved growth through demand innovation strategies suggests a number of guidelines from which other companies can learn. Here are six key principles that top executives can apply when developing new-growth initiatives, and that board members can use in evaluating and counseling the management teams of the companies they direct.

1. The Foundation: Operational Excellence

A company that is interested in developing a new-growth strategy must start by reexamining and reinforcing the strength of its core business. Paradoxical? Yes, but it's your core business that creates access to the arena of higher-order needs. No product sale, no related needs to serve. Having an efficient, profitable core business based on high-quality products and services will earn you permission from shareholders and customers to go farther.

Operational excellence also generates the funds you need to support new-growth initiatives. Take Cardinal Health as an example. Even as it developed expansive new enterprises over the past decade, Cardinal was steadily consolidating and improving the pharmaceutical distribution centers at the heart of its core business. Back in 1994, the company maintained forty distribution centers with average annual sales of $125 million each. Today, it operates only twenty-four centers with average annual sales of $1.4 billion or roughly triple the industry average. Cardinal plans to drive average center through-put to $2 billion over the next few years.

Every dollar saved on distribution costs becomes a dollar available for new-growth investment. This relentless focus on efficiency has allowed Cardinal to stay profitable *and* fund new growth even as overall industry gross margins have declined.

Thus, pursuing new growth is no excuse for neglecting core business excellence. Just the opposite: When launching new-growth initiatives, you need to redouble your operational diligence. But watch out for the trap at the other extreme—using the focus on core operations as an excuse to defer any serious new-growth moves. This can easily become a permanent state of mind, as management fixates on an end-less stream of quality and productivity initiatives, squeezing out ever-smaller returns from the same core business and neglecting the foundation of its future.

It's a delicate balancing act—a long-term discipline, not a onetime fix.

Bob Romasco is a CEO who has thought a lot about this balancing act. Between 1998 and 2001, he led a new-growth-based turnaround at Direct Marketing Services, (then a division of J. C. Penney, now owned by AEGON USA). Romasco sees most businesses as consisting of two big chunks: Unit A, which embodies the existing business model, and Unit B, which is inventing the future. Viewed schematically, the CEO's central challenge is to help Unit A find capital-creation activities that can throw off the income needed to support Unit B. In human terms, this means making it clear to everyone in the organization where they fit in this model *and letting them see their importance either way.*

"The guys in Unit A must never be made to feel that they are the stodgy, old-model folks who are being milked to support the hip, wave-of-the-future guys in Unit B," says Romasco. The CGO's job is to keep the big picture continually in focus and in balance—so that people can focus zealously on their more narrowly defined roles.

The focus on operating discipline can't stop at the margins of the base business. The best growth innovators bring careful discipline to new growth as well, tempering creativity and imagination with a structured process for identifying, assessing, and developing growth opportunities.

At Clarke American, for example, an annual process for developing new services is linked to a strategic vision blueprint that is updated every three to five years. In its Goal Development and Planning Process, Clarke American identifies specific action items and dates for completion, and the senior management team collectively tracks progress against this plan each month. As CEO Charles Korbell explains, "Clearly a big vision is important. But you need to back it down to, *What am I going to do* this year *in order to make progress?*"

2. The Grass Roots: Mandating New Growth at the Operating Level

Giving full responsibility for the growth challenge to a corporate strategy or business development team rarely works. Such teams usually lack the clout, operating experience, credibility, and funds needed to spearhead a real new-growth effort on their own. If you doubt this, think about your own company. Have you pulled several of your most dynamic and promising young executives from the operating units and asked them to staff your strategy or development group? When budget crunch time comes, is the funding of this group sacrosanct? Probably not.

At Cardinal Health, there is no corporate unit in charge of growing new businesses. Instead, everyone at the company from CEO Bob Walter on down builds the issue of growth into every day's decisions. As Walter explains, "Not only do you have to make strategy a part of your daily discipline, but strategy should also be defined by the operating managers, who are closest to the customer, supplier, industry relationships, and environment."

This sounds good in theory. But try calling the operating managers in your firm and asking them how much free time they have to devote to new-growth ideas. (We suggest holding the phone a few inches away from your ear when you do this.) So how does Cardinal get harried operating managers to focus on growth strategy?

One way is using measurements and incentives that hold operating mangers accountable for the growth of their businesses. The performance of every Cardinal manager is closely measured across two dimensions of growth—absolute growth and relative growth.

The *absolute* rate of growth is important because it supports overall financial health, generates profits to reinvest in the business, and helps attract and motivate the best talent. The *relative* rate of growth is important because Cardinal competes in the fast-growing healthcare sector. Growing at a high absolute rate while trailing the overall market's growth rate would not be acceptable at Cardinal. It would mean that over time, Cardinal would lose ground to competitors.

Of course, the combination of both measures is more meaningful than either alone. And in both dimensions, the level of growth demanded is what might be described as *realistic stretch*—challenging but achievable in the real-world business context. The fact that Cardinal is growing at over 15 percent per year, half again as fast as the industry average, is impressive. But that figure would not be a realistic target in an industry that is growing at only 2 percent per year—such as automobiles or steel. In those industries, a company pursuing new growth might set a goal of 4 to 5 percent, which is as ambitious in context as Cardinal's 15 percent. Setting unrealistic goals will only lead to failure, made worse by the bad moves your managers will make under excessive pressure.

Cardinal's unit managers know that they can't perform on the two key metrics of absolute growth and relative growth without a relentless focus on innovative sources of growth. The company's major growth initiatives—from automated drug delivery (Pyxis) to pharmacy management outsourcing to the packaging and sale of current market information to pharmaceutical manufacturers (ArcLight)—have all been developed and nurtured at the operational level. As a result, Cardinal has outgrown the overall healthcare distribution market by more than 50 percent annually (not including acquisitions).

Being in charge of growth is demanding and can be scary. It's also creative and energizing. Don't hoard the experience at the top executive level. Instead, distribute both the responsibility for growth and the opportunities to grow as widely as possible through your organization. When you do so, unexpected heroes and heroines are likely to emerge from the ranks.

3. A Thousand Flowers: Supporting Then Winnowing Maverick Ideas

It's not enough to encourage a culture of growth or even to support that culture through targeted metrics and incentives. Someone has to come up with the breakthrough ideas and translate them into real offerings, and bad ideas have to be killed quickly, before they consume significant time and money. How can senior managers unleash broader creativity to fuel next-generation growth while keeping new initiatives from multiplying uncontrollably?

The balancing act isn't easy. One CEO of a large manufacturing firm, which boasts a single highly visible new-growth initiative, struggles with the difficulty of maintaining his people's focus. "People tell me I need seven more initiatives like Project X," he complains. "That's a load of bull! There aren't seven more out there—not in our industry. Our key is to build out Project X from its current foothold and take full advantage of the opportunities it creates— not go chasing after new ventures that make no sense for us."

We spoke in a previous chapter about the value of the corporate antibodies that protect an organization from *bad* new ideas. One useful distinction the antibodies should make is between *scattering* innovation and *focusing* innovation.

Scattering innovation generates ideas with little concern for their economic feasibility or their relevance to customer needs or to one another. If acted upon, those ideas build fragmented business positions that are disconnected from one another and related only loosely to a company's assets. By contrast, focusing innovation generates ideas that coalesce in the spaces defined by customers' needs and the assets that provide a company with advantages. The company built through focusing innovation first lays down a new-growth foundation supported by a solid core of assets, then builds upon it, extending its scope gradually and methodically.

It's not about encouraging people to "go nuts," nor is it about "cracking down." What's needed is a balancing act: plenty of unfettered innovation, but within a defined space and making sound business sense.

Note that focused innovation does *not* mean making big all-or-nothing bets on radical service or technology breakthroughs. Most organizations and customer groups aren't ready for such moves; that's one reason they rarely succeed. Instead of shooting for the moon, create a new-business platform and look for steady, incremental opportunities that emerge from it, just as OnStar is expanding its offerings from security services to information and entertainment.

One effective model can be seen in Johnson Controls' approach to grassroots innovation. The firm encourages its people to spend time pursuing unconventional paths of inquiry, but it also imposes a staged evaluation process that separates winning ideas from losers and keeps the activity focused around its established business positions.

Jim Geschke, vice president and general manager of Electronics Integration, describes the process this way:

"Think of Johnson as an innovation machine. The front end has a robust series of gates that each idea must pass through. Early on, we'll have many ideas and spend a little money on each of them. As they get more fleshed out, the ideas go through a gate where a go/no-go decision is made. A lot of ideas get filtered out, so there are far fewer items and the spending on each goes up." In simple terms, the gate consists of a cross-functional team based within the business unit that meets periodically to discuss new ideas and review the progress of every initiative. This team makes the crucial funding decisions.

"Several months later," Geschke continues, "each idea will face another gate. If it passes, that means it's a serious idea that we are going to develop. Then the spending goes *way* up, and the number of ideas goes *way* down.

"By the time you reach the final gate, you need a credible business case in order to be accepted. At a certain point in the development process, we take our idea to customers and ask them what they think. Sometimes they say, 'That's a terrible idea, forget it.' Other times they say, 'That's fabulous, I want a million of them.' "

Notice that JCI's innovation process doesn't *start* with a customer survey, focus group, or other formalized feedback. It doesn't have to. JCI's engineers are working on-site with customers constantly and receive continual insights from the company's Core Customer Research unit. Being steeped in customer needs means that virtually every new-growth initiative launched at Johnson has at least some basis in customer reality.

Johnson gives people in the organization the latitude to push a project as far as it can go, even when customer demand isn't obvious. "HomeLink was an example of this," Geschke explains. "It was a product that no one directly asked for. But we recognized that in today's vehicles, the beautiful interiors are very harmonized, yet you've got this ugly appendage, the garage door opener, clipped on the visor. HomeLink is seamlessly integrated into the visor or the overhead console and is compatible with every garage door opener developed over the last thirty years. It was a significant challenge for us, and no customer asked for it. But we spent a few million dollars and hoped that the automakers would bite."

They did. HomeLink is now available on more than 150 different vehicle models from a wide range of automakers.

Having an idea turned back at a gate isn't viewed as a failure or a career setback. It's a common occurrence, and everyone knows that. "We really learn a lot from failing," Geschke explains. "So if you don't pass the gate, that's not viewed as a miss; that's viewed as a hit, because now we know what *not* to do.

"We embrace failure in general and we encourage people to fail *fast,* before the consequences are severe."

Is the Johnson system for innovation the only one or the best one? Not for every business. You need to tailor your gatekeeping techniques to the economic and marketplace realities of your own industry. Your new-growth process is every bit as important to your company's future as your manufacturing process or your financial analysis process, and it deserves the same kind of attention.

4. Running Interference: High-Level Support for Growth Initiatives

Most CEOs will tell you that growth is one of their top three priorities. Yet in terms of the time and energy they actually spend on various activities, growth usually ends up fifth or sixth. And most spend hardly any time on nurturing *new* forms of growth.

That's because new growth is hard. It involves leading the organization, the board, and even investors through uncomfortable forms of change. It requires active, ongoing commitment by senior managers who must be willing to visibly support the new business with their time, personal coaching, and political capital. The acid test is whether they are willing to ask parts of the organization to bear the pain of supporting the new initiative in some important way.

Consider three alternative approaches to building a new billion-dollar business and how those approaches are typically supported:

1. **New-product R&D.** An incumbent industrial firm pursuing this growth avenue usually creates a brand or product development team staffed with technically brilliant and creative people, develops a system for closely tracking and monitoring their work, and typically invests $300 million or more in the project. Chances of success: Good.
2. **Entrepreneurial start-up.** This growth approach usually involves a team of ten to thirty intensely dedicated, highly talented individuals working like crazy to bring a powerful personal vision to fruition. They are overseen by one or more venture-capital specialists experienced at building companies and armed with somewhere between $10 million and $100 million worth of investment money. Chances of success: Fair.
3. **New-growth initiative.** Most large companies attempting this approach assign half a dozen employees to the project. These are usually B players rather than the firm's best talent, they generally devote about half their time to the initiative, and senior management's direct involvement is minimal. Corporate investment ranges between zero and a few million dollars. Chances of success: Close to zero.

If you're a trifle skeptical about your company's new-growth prospects, measure your past investment in growth initiatives against this scale. Which picture is closest to your company's practice? Does this help to explain your track record?

New-growth initiatives deserve resources commensurate with their importance. Most large companies spend hundreds of millions, if not billions of dollars on product R&D without any certainty as to which spending will produce revenues or when it will happen. By contrast, most new-growth initiatives are starved for funding, subjected to onerous budget reviews, and held to impossibly high standards of certainty about their payback potential.

Companies can't afford to invest willy-nilly. But as CGO, you should consider devoting 10 to 15 percent of your product innovation budget to customer innovation instead.

Cardinal Health has done this through a unique system for funding innovation known as *strategic spending*. This involves a pool of money contributed by every division in the corporation from which specific new-growth initiatives are funded. Jim Millar, the COO of Cardinal's distribution business, explains it by an example. "We came up with an idea for letting our hospital customers combine their pharmaceutical and medical-surgical purchases. Even outside suppliers are drawn into this loop.

"Now, setting up this new system required investment—creating an organization, hiring people, and so on. But since it cut across several Cardinal businesses, it was hard to get any one division to fund it.

So we went to strategic spending and got the seed money to launch the initiative. By next year, the new business will build its own revenue base, and both the costs and the income will be distributed among all the divisions involved."

Millar notes two important features of the strategic spending approach. To start, the investment pool is funded *first* off the top of each year's budget. Second, the pervasive growth culture within Cardinal limits political intrigue over the allocation of investment funds. "There's not much jealousy about which projects get funded, because we all have a stake in Cardinal's success," Millar explains. "And anyway, if you resent paying into the fund without drawing money from it, then shame on you! It means you're not being creative enough to come up with new ideas for the fund to support."

Just as important as financial support is comprehensive senior management support in the form of time, energy, and political capital. At many companies, new-growth initiatives have senior executive champions in the early, heady days when the business is all promise and no one has had to make any tough decisions or allocate scarce dollars and talent. Few can point to the kind of ongoing commitment provided to OnStar by GM's then current senior management team, including Chairman Jack Smith, CEO Rick Wagoner, Vice Chairman Harry Pierce, and Ron Zarrella, head of GM North America. Their commitment was manifested in three ways.

- First, they were willing to provide significant funding to build the business over an extended number of years and in the face of significant competing demands.
- Second, they were willing to disrupt activities of the core business on OnStar's behalf, most notably by interceding in vehicle development schedules (sacrosanct territory at GM) to accelerate factory installation of OnStar components.
- Third, they gave hours of their own time and plenty of personal energy to the new business—for instance, by arranging introductions to their counterparts at other automakers to discuss installing OnStar in their vehicles.

If you're a top executive, you know that every move you make or don't make is freighted with enormous symbolic importance for everyone in the company. After flashing the green light on new-growth initiatives, how much of your own time and energy have you invested in them? How strongly have you encouraged their leaders, and (when necessary) how hard have you pushed?

If you want to get serious about new growth, take meaningful, visible steps to nurture these initiatives. Talk about them, probe for signs of progress or problems, and back up your words with time, energy, and money. And be persistent, even beyond what may appear to be "reasonable." Get into the habit of asking, "What can we do to go *faster*?"

Bob Romasco of Direct Marketing Services learned the importance of persistence in trying to market a new-business initiative within an organization. Determined to win the front-line workers as allies, he became the first CEO in company history to make regular visits to a separately housed production facility. After he'd visited the department to push his mandate for change for the *eighth* time, one worker casually told him, "You know, I'm starting to think you're serious about this."

Yes, it may take eight visits before your own people take you seriously. Be prepared for that—and when you make the new-growth commitment, be ready to back it up.

5. Form and Function: Structuring the New-Growth Business

Next-generation opportunities are often fundamentally different from your core business, with different economics, capital structure, and methods of capturing value. To succeed, these businesses need to be understood and structured in this light. Obvious? Maybe—but most companies have spent a lot of time and effort creating common metrics, rewards, titles, pay grades, and organizational structures in order to better align their organizations. The last thing most senior managers want to do is open up the Pandora's box of exceptions. So there's usually strong resistance to the necessity of establishing different structures for new-growth businesses. But make no mistake—it *is* a necessity.

As a new addition to Deere & Company, John Deere Landscapes differs greatly from its parent company in almost every element of its business model, including the nature of the products sold, the place within the value chain, and the overall economic equation.

In response to these differences, JDL President Dave Werning and the executive team at Deere have worked hard to distinguish JDL from the core equipment business. JDL was launched with a tacit agreement establishing a wall between it and the rest of Deere that contains a "one-way window." Werning and his lieutenants can look into Deere and borrow ideas and use resources, but the reverse is discouraged. Thus, at least during its initial growth phase, JDL is operating independently from most of the parent company's traditional equipment-centric processes.

The one-way window works in some small but important ways. Some of the big-company processes that work well in other parts of Deere do not offer the same advantages to JDL, which prides itself on its entrepreneurial mind-set. "We find we can sometimes do things cheaper than our parent company," Werning says, "and saving every penny is essential for a start-up, especially in the distribution business. So I try to maintain separate systems for purchasing, human resources, and other administrative tasks. I'm proud of the fact that I sit in chairs that I previously used in a different unit way back in 1991. They were owned by Deere, which was planning to scrap them. I said, 'We'll take them—they're fully depreciated.'

That's the way a distribution company has to be run."

For Johnson Controls, the structural challenge was very different. Here, the critical goal was to integrate the new business into the old, creating a new companywide systems capability that fused customer understanding with know-how related to specific auto components. Johnson's response was to rebuild the entire organization as a matrix defined along two dimensions. Customer Business Units are geared toward meeting the needs of a particular client: There's a DaimlerChrysler unit, a Toyota unit, and so on. Product Business Units oversee specific types of product, such as interior components, seating units, and electronics.

Although the Customer Business Units are primarily geared toward marketing while Product Business Units are geared toward engineering, design, and production, the functions are allowed to overlap, promoting the free flow of information throughout the company. Thus, the restructuring of JCI was directly driven by underlying business logic, especially the need to cross-fertilize customer insight with engineering knowledge.

Yet another approach is seen at Clarke American, where the central challenge was to combine its product and service offerings into an integrated system designed to maximize the overall profitability of Clarke American's banking partners. To achieve this, Clarke American reorganized by customer segment, changing its accounting and incentive systems to measure customer profitability (not product profitability) and even creating redundant service functions such as finance and information technology within each customer unit.

Whether your new-growth effort involves redirecting the entire firm or creating an offshoot from your core business, don't simply replicate existing structures, however effective they may be. Once again: *New growth has different needs.*

6. Missing Pieces: Building the Asset Base Through Acquisitions and Alliances

Many companies that decide to pursue new-growth opportunities try to do it entirely with homegrown resources. In human terms, this means that responsibility may be given to strong performers who are already stretched thin or to people who have been passed over for other opportunities and may be mediocre performers.

In terms of hard assets, companies often try to make do with capabilities they already own rather than building new ones or looking outside the company for necessary assets. The underlying impulse toward thrift and efficiency is understandable and correct; it's important to save money by using available assets when possible. (Dave Werning's ten-year-old office chairs come to mind.) But most new-growth businesses require people and assets that differ from those in the core business in some important way—puzzle pieces that may be small in themselves but are essential to completing the picture. Selective acquisitions can fill this gap.

Notice the difference between traditional acquisitions and the kinds of acquisitions needed to support growth moves. The former, which might be dubbed *revenue acquisitions,* are usually focused on building scale to create revenue growth and cost synergies. A typical example would be a bank buying another bank and thereby expanding both its customer base and its geographic reach. Revenue acquisitions tend to grab headlines and dominate the annual lists of biggest corporate deals, yet they have a discouraging track record when measured in terms of sustained growth.

By contrast, the acquisitions that matter most in the new-growth context might be called *capability acquisitions.* They serve to speed development, bring in required skills, open doors to strategic markets, and otherwise improve the odds of success for a new-growth initiative. Though a well-planned capability acquisition may be small in dollar value, it can serve as the essential kernel around which a major new business is built.

Examples of powerful capability acquisitions include:

- Johnson Controls' 1996 acquisition of Prince, which added not only a set of valuable electronics technologies but also a finely honed managerial mechanism with a proven track record of technical innovation.
- Cardinal Health's 1996 acquisition of Pyxis, which

gave it a leading position in the automated delivery of pharmaceutical products along with greatly expanded capabilities for capturing, tracking, analyzing, and communicating drug-related health-care data.

• John Deere Landscapes' 2001 acquisition of Richton International, which gave it a position in the irrigation equipment market critical to fulfilling its one-stop-shop service vision.

The key to planning smart capability acquisitions is to focus on the invisible balance sheet and look for purchases that will help maximize the value of any hidden assets while neutralizing or overcoming hidden liabilities.

Of course, buying a company outright isn't the only way of building an asset base. Alliances can also provide access to key capabilities, as when GM On-Star arranged for other automakers to install OnStar on their vehicles and when it contracted with outside suppliers such as General Magic and XM Radio to provide content services to OnStar subscribers.

Yet another way of expanding the asset base is through the hiring of individuals who bring new skill sets. When OnStar needed to quickly develop capabilities in technological fields that were unfamiliar to General Motors' traditional engineering corps (software, the Internet, database management), the company hired a platoon of veterans from Silicon Valley.

The Preflight Checklist

Executing new-growth strategies will never be easy. That's true by definition, since a new-growth initiative is a discovery expedition into unknown territory. The ideas presented in this chapter are principles of navigation. Only you can decide where these principles should take you and your company.

Given the challenges and dangers associated with getting new-growth efforts off the ground, every organization that is preparing to embark on one needs to ensure it's prepared before taking off. Consider the following questions your preexpedition checklist.

- [ ] Is there a clearly committed and talented day-to-day leader for the new business?
- [ ] Will your senior management team invest their precious time, resources, and political clout to support it?
- [ ] Are there ten high-quality people you are willing to send to staff it?
- [ ] Are you willing to hire additional key senior team members as needed?
- [ ] Are you prepared to enter into alliances to provide the capabilities and resources as needed?
- [ ] Are you ready to support the new business unit with its own profit and loss statement and an off-site location if appropriate?
- [ ] Are you willing to authorize a significant level of budget authority once the initial concept is proven financially sound?

☐ Are you prepared to develop and apply to the new business a set of different performance metrics and a different compensation formula than those used in the core business?

If you can't answer Yes for every item above, you should probably abort your new-growth initiative for now . . . and use the Nos to drive your to-do list for the months to come.

PART FOUR

Opportunities on the
Growth Frontier

13

Decoding the Economics of
Consumers: Progressive Insurance,
DeWolfe Homeowner Services,
and Mobil Speedpass

Walk into any U.S. supermarket and you feel you've arrived on the planet of plenty. The place seems to go on for miles, aisle after aisle bursting with color and visual appeal. Even in a category as esoteric as salsa, there are nearly a dozen varieties available, conveniently packaged to whatever specifications you desire. And to dip in them you've got dozens of snack foods to choose from, from tortilla chips to baked plantain wafers.

The supermarket isn't unique. At the clothing boutique down the street, outfits in dozens of styles, colors, and combinations are on display. The bookstore two doors down boasts ten thousand titles. The hardware store in a nearby shopping center offers twenty kinds of screwdrivers.

It looks like a consumer paradise. But behind the shelves of plenty lurks a not-so-cheerful economic reality. Companies selling consumer products and services have been *too* successful at creating new offerings for the marketplace. Now they're paying the price.

Welcome to the Quagmire

The blunt reality is that consumer companies face even bleaker growth prospects than their business-to-business counterparts. In fact, they've been in a growth crisis for some time. Less than 3 percent of consumer companies have enjoyed double-digit growth for at least eight of the past ten years, compared to 7 percent of all companies.

Some of the country's most venerable firms are stuck in this drought. Procter & Gamble has a 0 percent core revenue growth rate (after subtracting international, M&A, and price-based growth). Gillette, –0.1 percent. McDonald's, –2.1 percent. MetLife, 1.0 percent. And they're all doing better than ConAgra, which is currently experiencing a –2.3 percent core revenue growth rate.

And don't think consumer companies can pin their hopes on increased customer spending. It's just not going to happen. Over the past decade, consumer spending grew at an average annual rate of just 3.3 percent, with about three-quarters of that growth in nondiscretionary purchases such as food and shelter. Discretionary items including movie tickets and travel amount to less than a sixth of all consumer spending—and they hardly grew at all.

All the while, consumer-oriented companies have deluged this space with a dizzying and ever-expanding array of product and service offerings. Thanks to new channels such as the Internet and direct mail, the number of credit card carriers, home equity lenders, and life insurers competing for consumer business has mushroomed . . . while their offers blur in a sea of junk mail.

The frenzy of simultaneous product launches means that the vast majority are doomed. Those that succeed face diminished prospects in a crowded market. With ever-greater competition for a limited supply of dollars and attention, is there any hope for sustained growth for consumer products companies?

Roadblocks Ahead

We've already seen how business-to-business companies can achieve new levels of growth by addressing customers' higher-order needs. Can the same strategy work for consumer companies? Yes—but the higher-order needs of consumers are often profoundly different from those experienced by businesses.

Consumers are driven by many kinds of ideas and emotions. Most of us yearn for the peace of mind and the feeling of security that a favored brand can give. We enjoy the sense of self-definition that comes from choosing and using products that reflect our personalities, and we crave both a feeling of connection to others and a sense of individual superiority. These and other semiconscious desires are reflected in the cars we drive, the jeans we wear, and the beers we drink.

But not all of the higher-order needs of consumers are emotional. Consumers also have some of the same sorts of practical higher-order needs as businesses. While individuals don't keep balance sheets and profit and loss statements, they do have budgets, schedules, and the need to juggle both in an increasingly complicated world. So consumers, like businesses, want more efficiency, streamlining, and ease of use in the products and services they buy.

These are important higher-order needs, and consumers are willing to reward companies that effectively address them. Indeed, finding ways to meet such demands can provide consumer companies with an unprecedented opportunity to build loyalty, differentiate their offerings, expand their market opportunities, and create ways to capture value. Yet few consumer companies have seized this opportunity.

In this chapter, we'll look at several consumer companies that have succeeded in leveraging their hidden assets to improve the customer experience, removing hassles and needless costs from daily life. Some have taken relatively simple steps to enhance their product or service, thus stealing market share and expanding their margins. Others have leveraged their assets in more radical ways, opening up entirely new business opportunities.

Slippery When Wet

Progressive Insurance has focused intensely on understanding and eliminating a major source of frustration and anxiety for car owners. In doing so, it has carved out a unique position in the otherwise undifferentiated auto insurance marketplace. Not coincidentally, it has also grown faster and more profitably than its competitors.

To understand what Progressive does for its customers, consider the story of thirty-two-year-old Brenda Hopkins. Nearly two years ago, Hopkins was driving home from her parents' house outside Norman, Oklahoma, when a summer thunderstorm rolled in over the plain. Through her rain-streaked windshield, she made out the shape of a yellow Chevy Impala stopped on the right-hand side of an upcoming intersection. *That's fine,* she thought. *He's waiting for me to pass.*

She was wrong. Just seconds before Hopkins entered the intersection, the driver of the Chevy abruptly accelerated straight into her path. Hopkins barely had time to react as the yellow flash registered in her peripheral vision. Veering left, she clipped the front end of the Impala and spun skidding through the intersection, flattened a stand of cottonwood saplings, and came to rest upright in a ditch.

Fortunately, no one was seriously hurt. Hopkins's vehicle was another matter. The 1999 Ford Explorer had sustained major damage to the right front quarter, the radiator had been punctured, and the front axle had been bent in the ditch.

Having been in a crash once before, Hopkins knew what to expect from the claims process. First, her car would be towed to a garage. Then she would have to wait while her insurance company scheduled a visit by its adjuster to study the damage and authorize repairs. Only then, days later, would the garage begin work. Most likely, the garage would then uncover more damage that hadn't been visible at first, so the insurance company would have to schedule another appointment for the adjuster to approve the additional work. It would be a long, painful process punctuated by paperwork and bureaucratic hassles. Meanwhile, Hopkins would be waiting on street corners for buses or hitching rides with her neighbors.

That night, sitting in a police cruiser by her wrecked car in the driving rain, she just wanted her life back.

But Hopkins was in for a pleasant surprise. Six months before, she had changed insurance companies. She called her new carrier, Progressive. Within an hour of her accident, Hopkins was shaking hands with a Progressive assessor, who arrived on the scene in a company van, ascertained the extent of the damage, approved the necessary repairs, and cut her a check on the spot.

"Because the garage was able to start work right away," she now says, "I got my car back in four days—and that was including the time it took to order a part that the garage did not have in stock.

The whole incident was traumatic, but I know it would have been worse if Progressive hadn't been so proactive in processing my claim."

The Best of the Worst

Brenda Hopkins's experience, replicated tens of thousands of times, is the reason that Progressive has grown to become the fourth-largest auto insurance company in the United States, serving five million households. Progressive stands out not because its coverage is different but because it is the best at helping customers through the most traumatic and hassle-filled experience associated with car ownership.

Founded in 1937 in Cleveland, Ohio, Progressive long specialized in writing policies for the kinds of customers most other insurers avoid: drunk drivers, the elderly, non–English speakers, drivers with histories of frequent accidents, even those with criminal records for fraud. This so-called nonstandard market is treacherous terrain, but Progressive prospered and grew because it carefully chose its customers from among the ranks of the undesirable and then focused on managing its risk exposure.

Given the nature of its customer base, Progressive knew that it had to be particularly careful to guard against fraud. So it learned to conduct its claim assessments quickly and thoroughly, dispatching adjusters promptly to the scene of an accident for timely firsthand appraisal of what had occurred.

Quick customer service also allowed Progressive to settle a claim quickly and cheaply, before a victim's attorney could get involved. As a by-product, it earned the loyalty of customers who appreciated Progressive's prompt service.

The success of Progressive's approach was evident in its financial results. By 1990, it was one of the few insurance companies in the country making a profit on the policies it was writing. While the auto insurance industry as a whole lost 8.5 cents on every underwriting dollar, Progressive was posting a profit of 5.6 cents per dollar.

Progressive had been forced to learn how to survive in an unforgiving climate. Now it was prepared to leverage its crucial skills in more lucrative and competitive markets.

Going Big

At the same time, it was becoming clear that the high-risk auto insurance market wouldn't sustain Progressive's growth forever. Not only was the size of the market shrinking, but mainstream insurers such as Allstate and State Farm were beginning to encroach on its terrain by writing more policies to riskier customers.

And so in 1991, Progressive decided to reach beyond the nonstandard market into the much larger world of standard and preferred auto insurance. The move would expand Progressive's potential market space more than sixfold, from $18 billion to $120 billion.

Progressive's fast and comprehensive claims management service, which had been essential to its survival in the high-risk market, would now become the crucial hidden asset that would enable it to trump the competition in the standard/preferred market. It would bring its expertise and network of assessors to average auto insurance customers, who had long endured the hassles, loss of time, and stress associated with collecting on an insurance policy.

Scaling up its infrastructure devised to serve the high-risk market, Progressive promised to have a company representative at the scene of an accident within two hours. Progressive has continued to engineer its customer service. In 1994, it introduced a fleet of fifteen hundred "Immediate Response Vehicles" equipped with laptop computers, intelligent software, and wireless access to the company's claims department. As a result, Progressive is both cutting costs and earning high ratings for customer satisfaction.

"We focus a tremendous amount of effort on our claims organization. Claims represent 75 percent of our cost structure," says a Progressive executive. "Any process improvement we can make in claims has tremendous leverage in improving our profitability. The insurance company that has the best claims organization will become the biggest insurer."

Progressive's move into the broader auto insurance market coincided with a downturn in that industry. Owing to severe competition for market share and increased opportunities for comparison-shopping by consumers, premium growth industry-wide slowed from 4.9 percent from 1993–1998 to 0.7 percent in 2000. Yet Progressive has thrived because of its connection with consumers' broader needs. It has generated underwriting profits in eight out of the past ten years, with top-line growth averaging 18.3 percent.

The Hassles of Home Buying

As Benjamin Franklin observed, moving twice is about as bad as having your house burn down once. The ordeal of moving hasn't gotten any easier, but Americans won't kick the habit. Each year, one American in eight packs up and moves.

Americans' peripatetic ways have been good to The DeWolfe Companies of Lexington, Massachusetts. DeWolfe has used its focus on the higher-order needs associated with home buying and moving not only to differentiate its Realty business but also to gain access to new opportunities in adjacent markets.

Founded in 1949 as a family-run brokerage in the suburbs of Boston, DeWolfe grew through a series of acquisitions. In 1992, it became the first real estate company in the United States to go public, which provided the capital to expand its geographic reach and service offerings.

By 2002, DeWolfe had nearly a hundred retail offices and more than three thousand sales agents and employees, along with a dominant position in the lucrative New England real estate market. But it hasn't been content to stop with geographic expansion.

Through its close working relationships with both buyers and sellers, DeWolfe saw an opportunity to help address the hassles that plague prospective home buyers. Buying a home combines complex, opaque processes with a sobering financial commitment. It's often accompanied by a major life transition—marriage or divorce, the birth of a child, a new job or retirement. There are multiple parties—Realtors, lawyers, insurers, bankers, and movers—who all need to be chosen and coordinated. And to make matters worse, many decisions are nested: The purchase agreement can't be finalized until the bank authorizes the loan; the loan can't be approved until the house is chosen and appraised; and the loan can't be finalized until the insurance is obtained. The result is a labyrinth of unfamiliar "to dos" that's at best confusing, at worst nightmarish.

DeWolfe recognized a significant opportunity to provide customers with a much less painful home-buying experience. Its solution was to provide all the necessary services under one roof. Doing so would address a major source of customer frustration and also would open up new sales opportunities in mortgages, insurance, and moving services.

DeWolfe was uniquely suited to tackling this problem because of its market position. In the home-buying process, the Realtor is ideally positioned to string several services together, because the real estate purchase catalyzes the need for all the other services. Consumers don't choose their property insurance provider and then begin looking for a house; the house deal comes first. However, because the home purchase requires certification of insurance, it's natural for the real estate broker to serve as a clearinghouse for property insurance.

The same is true with financing. Loan preapproval helps consumers in bidding for properties, especially in hot markets where it's essential to get the bid in quickly. So the first thing many real estate agents do is steer the customer into the preapproval process. Again, the agent is the first point of contact and the guide through the labyrinth.

Beginning in 1986, DeWolfe began building a full-service mortgage lending operation. With a mortgage consultant in every real estate office, the company quickly established a foothold in its customers' financing business. DeWolfe Mortgage built its processing capabilities to ensure that the mortgage wouldn't hold up the real estate closing and established relationships with multiple lenders to offer its customers more than two hundred mortgage products.

In 1996, DeWolfe followed this up by entering the insurance business. Now, when a home purchase agreement is signed, licensed insurance specialists help the customer secure homeowner's insurance, arrange for the binder to arrive in time for the closing, and review home warranty, auto, and umbrella coverage options.

In 2000, DeWolfe took its latest step, entering the moving business. Having negotiated preferred rates and service agreements with van lines, DeWolfe can provide move coordination and assistance once a purchase agreement is signed.

Don't confuse DeWolfe's business model with the kind of cross-sell play that financial services firms so often pursue, usually with limited success. Most cross-sell efforts fail because the consumer gets no real added value from buying the products or services as a bundle. By contrast, by coordinating a collection of home-buying services in one place, the DeWolfe offer reduces the number of customer touch points in the process, increases speed and accuracy, and reduces hassles and anxiety.

DeWolfe's customers approve. By 2001, 40 percent of DeWolfe's brokerage customers also obtained their mortgages and insurance through the company. Revenues from mortgage and insurance services nearly doubled over the past three years, and revenues from moving services are growing at more than 50 percent per year.

Interestingly, while 79 percent of customers who used DeWolfe to buy a home said they were "very satisfied" or "extremely satisfied" with their experience, the rate rose to 93 percent among those who also financed and insured their home with DeWolfe. Explains CEO Richard DeWolfe, "Our core customer values the convenience and consistent quality of integrated service delivery, embodied by our 'one stop and you're home' business model."

By expanding its services to include all the critical steps in the home-buying process, DeWolfe has not only differentiated its brokerage business but also has increased its potential market space dramatically. As a broker, it played in a New England real estate brokerage market worth $1.5 billion. Just by expanding into mortgages and home insurance, DeWolfe's opportunity more than doubled, to $3.8 billion. And these new revenues are recurring. While house buyers pay a commission on a new purchase just once every seven years on average, they make mortgage and insurance payments year in and year out. The new revenue streams mitigate the cyclicality of the real estate brokerage business.

Overall, DeWolfe's revenues and profit have gone up more than 400 percent over the past five years. Today it is the largest home ownership company in New England, with a 10 percent real estate market share, a service share approaching 33 percent, and an overall customer satisfaction rating of 82 percent.

In business, there is no sincerer form of flattery than a large cash payment. In August 2002, the national real estate colossus NRT (a division of Cendant) announced a cash tender offer for DeWolfe that valued the company at a 100 percent premium over its pre-offer stock price. DeWolfe's business model will now be available for replication across Cendant's larger nationwide Coldwell Banker brokerage business.

The Tao of Growth

Going beyond Progressive, DeWolfe sought to use its focus on serving consumers' next-generation needs to expand to multiple adjacent markets. Mobil Oil took an even more radical step by leveraging a hidden asset to create potential growth through a totally new business while at the same time reengineering its core consumer operation.

In the early 1990s, ExxonMobil was vexed by the so-called right-hand-turn syndrome. Most gasoline customers don't discriminate by brand; they'll turn off the road to buy gas at whichever station happens to be closest when their tank runs low. Mobil needed to find a way to increase differentiation and, thus, to lure drivers to their outlets. It also needed to offset declining revenues in its core gasoline retailing business by increasing sales at its profitable minimart outlets.

In talking with its customers, Mobil learned that many of them felt that visiting a gas station involved too much hassle. Consumers saw filling up as a dirty and unpleasant chore. As a rule, they bought gas while en route to somewhere else; so the less time they spent at the pump, the better.

Mobil responded to the customers' message. Working with Texas Instruments, Mobil created Speedpass, a tiny electronic transponder that could be waved near a receiver-transmitter at a gas pump or minimart cash register and instantly trigger a secure credit card transaction in the holder's name. Since the system is set up for preapproved small transactions (less than $50), there is no need for the usual credit or balance checks. The result is an approximate saving of forty-five seconds for the customer at the pump. (If that doesn't sound like much, look at your watch and consciously tick off the time. In today's speeded-up world, forty-five seconds can feel like an eternity when it's spent standing at the gas pump.)

Introduced in 1997, Speedpass was an instant success. Soon it was integrated into the ExxonMobil convenience stores and the new "On the Run" stores, making buying food and sundries on the road quick and effortless. Early results indicate that Speedpass customers are twice as loyal as the average customer—in fact, Mobil credits Speedpass with a 2.5 percent increase in gas sales during 2000.

In meeting its customers' higher-order need for efficiency, Mobil captured both the value of increased purchases and longer-term customer loyalty. But the opportunity for Mobil goes beyond its core gas business. Speedpass now has five million users—a number that is expected to grow to thirty million by 2007. This installed base of users represents a huge new hidden asset, a group of customers whose loyalty will hereafter be tightly tied to Mobil, and a potential basis for creating a de facto standard for cashless transactions.

Mobil has already begun to focus on exploiting this latter opportunity. In the United States alone, the volume of small cash transactions—including fast food, convenience store, vending machine, and other small purchases—totals more than $400 billion annually. There are several opportunities associated with improving transaction efficiencies in this market. For the consumer, the advantage is that the average cashier transaction takes just ten to fifteen seconds—far faster than your average debit or credit card transaction—and they don't need to worry about having cash on hand before entering the store. For retailers, cashless payment systems can increase purchase frequency and average ticket size while reducing "shrinkage" due to employee theft. And Mobil will earn a transaction processing fee on purchases made with Speedpass, while also earning the float on consumers' purchase balances.

The most widely deployed approach for cashless transactions is the bank debit card, but the transactions are slow and expensive to process and may involve out-of-network ATM fees for consumers. Speedpass is quick, the back-end processing system is already up and running, and its five million users gives it important critical mass.

Mobil has begun to license Speedpass for use at McDonald's and other fast-food chains and retailers. After an initial trial, the program was expanded to cover more than four hundred McDonald sites in the Chicago area, and plans for a wider rollout are being worked out.

And there's more to come. Mobil has announced that Stop & Shop Supermarkets started testing Speedpass at selected stores in fall 2002, with a new feature built in: linkage of consumers' Stop & Shop loyalty card to Speedpass. When Stop & Shop customers use Speedpass to pay for groceries, they instantly get Stop & Shop discounts and rewards while simultaneously paying for their purchase.

In creating Speedpass, Mobil's original aims were to solve its customers' need for a quicker, easier, more hassle-free gasoline transaction and to create some basis for differentiation in a commodity marketplace. Now Speedpass has now become a business opportunity in its own right—a potentially vast and lucrative one. The challenge for Mobil will be balancing its desire to preserve the differentiation of its gasoline purchasing experience with the opportunity to set an industry standard—which means making Speedpass available to competitors.

That's the thing about growth opportunities: Once you tap into one, you never know where it might take you. But any company stuck in a no-growth zone would be happy to face a dilemma similar to Mobil's.

14

Touching the Consumer's Softer Side: Virgin, Kodak, and Intuit

Progressive, DeWolfe, and Mobil each prospered by studying the customer process surrounding their product or service transaction and then making it easier, faster, and more pleasant. Each created a new basis for differentiation and growth, in part because they interacted directly with customers and were involved in relatively complex purchase or ownership experiences.

But many consumer companies don't enjoy such a direct relationship with their customers. In categories such as food, health and beauty items, consumer electronics, and clothing, large and increasingly powerful retailers own the transaction—and hence the opportunity to serve the broader consumer needs surrounding the product. Where it is even possible, attempts to circumvent these middlemen can be risky.

Even when consumer product companies do manage to reach out directly to the end user, the modest price and complexity of their products and the straightforward ways in which they're used leave few opportunities to reengineer the consumer experience to tap large latent needs. For example, it's doubtful whether a cereal maker could fundamentally alter the small, routine nature of purchasing and consuming cornflakes.

Furthermore, compared to their counterparts in the business-to-business sector, most consumer product companies know little about their individual customers. There are far too many of them. And the cost to reach and serve consumers in most of these categories is high relative to the average revenue per customer.

Is the notion of next-generation needs relevant in these categories? Are there opportunities to create new avenues of growth by serving customers in new and innovative ways despite these hardships?

The answer to both these questions is yes—if you think creatively about how to get around these problems and are willing to think differently about the customer and the nature of higher-order needs. Companies like Virgin, Kodak, and Intuit, among others, provide examples of several of the ways to find new growth amid these challenging circumstances.

Like a Virgin

Virgin has forged a record of remarkable growth by taking over a series of markets—markets connected not by product similarities but by their customers' willingness to embrace a carefully crafted Virgin lifestyle. In the process, the company has exploited the fact that an enormous gap exists between corporate and individual purchasing psychology. That gap can be summed up in a single word: *emotion.*

Companies purchase products and services because they are deemed essential to the processes of the enterprise. By contrast, consumers often make purchases to meet needs that are primarily emotional. One of the strongest of these needs is the desire to belong and to have your sense of self affirmed and proclaimed to others. Virgin has established itself as an affinity hub, a symbolic standard-bearer for a youthful, vivacious way of life that embraces fresh styles and a spirit of cheeky independence in travel, music, communications, and clothing. Empowered by its customers' loyalty, it has been able to expand its offerings into a diverse range of products and services. Its shared sense of identity with its customers has let it connect with them on many fronts.

As an example of how Virgin affinity works, consider the case of twenty-three-year-old Londoner Sharon Eggleston. Growing up in the heart of the city, Eggleston came of age among the world's first techno-literate youth generation, a group that considers high-speed, high-bandwidth telecommunications its birthright.

All of Eggleston's friends already had cell phones, along with beepers, digital pagers, and all the other stylish high-tech accoutrements of the Internet Age. But she was frustrated by the cell phone subscription plans being offered. All were structured along the same lines, with difficult-to-understand payment systems that required hefty upfront payments, sizable minimum calling charges, and larcenous roaming fees that didn't suit her lifestyle or cash flow. After looking into the matter for a few weeks, Eggleston threw in the towel. She felt as if the phone companies were alien, vaguely sinister conspiracies dedicated to making her life miserable.

Eggleston's frustration turned to hope one afternoon when she spotted a billboard advertising a new cellular service provider—Virgin Mobile. Had the company carried any other name, Eggleston's eyes might have glazed over. But the Virgin brand meant something to her. It meant cool. Young. Affordable. Efficient, yet fun. Virgin, in short, was the kind of company that she could identify with and trust.

The brand name caught Eggleston's eye, and the plan's prices and structure—emphasizing pay-as-you-go charges rather than hefty monthly fees—won her over. Today, excellent service and a sense of community keep her a happy customer. "It's been great," she says. "Somehow, given the Virgin name, I knew it would be."

Eggleston didn't realize it, but when she signed up for a Virgin phone, she was buying more than a cellular service. She was buying a sense of identity and belonging. She was becoming a Virgin customer.

The Young Ones

The Virgin Group has enjoyed a powerful bond with the youth culture ever since the 1970s, when a fun-loving yet passionately determined nineteen-year-old named Richard Branson decided to start a mail-order record company and name it after his own lack of experience in the business world.

The tiny start-up grew to be a powerhouse record company, then branched out into a host of widely divergent enterprises. Thirty-five years later, Virgin is a loosely linked family of twenty-nine companies ranging from such sizable operations as Virgin Atlantic Airlines and Virgin Megastores to tiny Virgin Limobike, a motorcycle passenger service. This is no dysfunctional conglomerate family: Over the past decade, the group has grown at a compound annual rate of 12 percent, to more than $6 billion in sales in 2002 . . . in markets that are mostly bumping along with mid-single-digit growth.

Richard Branson's genius lies in creating a brand identity that relates not to the product or service on offer, but to the lifestyle aspirations of its customers. Virgin's seemingly unrelated businesses all share the same spirit of youthful exuberance and joie de vivre. Youth, energy, and success are things we all admire, and by linking ourselves to Virgin as customers we can hope to somehow embody them. Branson's style has helped create an identifiable corporate personality with which consumers can feel a personal bond.

The virtue of this approach is that it creates an image generalized enough to apply to virtually any product or service, allowing access in principle to an unlimited growth field. At first glance—or even at second glance—the airline business seems to have nothing to do with the record business. Yet the Virgin strategy makes them fit together.

By contrast, if Virgin Records' original brand identity had been built around some novel musical sound or other product-centered attribute, the company's leap into commercial aviation would have seemed truly random. But when Virgin took to the skies, it promised to bring a spirit of freshness and verve. The message appealed to consumers frustrated by the delays, poor service, and opaque pricing schemes of the traditional airlines. Virgin Atlantic didn't dilute the Virgin brand; it enhanced it by offering a zesty and efficient service that perfectly matched the Virgin image. In addition to the usual airline fare of movie and an entrée, for instance, Virgin Atlantic also offers onboard massages and a wet bar.

The same is true of other Virgin enterprises. By crafting a brand identity that appeals to its customers' need for affinity, Virgin has created an image that can embrace virtually any product or service, from finance to soft drinks, wines to holiday packages, and publishing to mobile phones—each a business that Virgin has successfully launched. Consumers are so trusting of the Virgin name that they will allow the company to reach out and connect with them in virtually any market segment. The result is a set of new-growth opportunities that go well beyond what mere product or brand extensions would have allowed Virgin to achieve.

Contrast Virgin's affinity-branding approach with traditional branding, where the image is closely linked to a product's positive attributes. Tide laundry detergent is one of America's best-known and respected brands. It exerts unquestioned authority in its category; everyone knows that Tide means clean, fresh, and economical. Yet its authority is narrowly limited to the realm of cleaning clothes. Tide could logically expand into laundry additives or perhaps even washing machines, but a Tide clothing shop or a Tide auto service center would only furrow eyebrows.

On the Prowl

Virgin's message is about more than belonging. A crucial aspect of the brand is its reputation for products and services that are easier, cheaper, and more fun. The company's strategy is to identify a market with a sizable population of disappointed, frustrated consumers and figure out a way to improve the offer. "We look for opportunities where we can offer something better, fresher, and more valuable, and we seize them," a company statement says. "We often move into areas where the customer has traditionally received a poor deal and where the competition is complacent."

Given the perceived incompetence of the incumbents in the cell phone business, Virgin wasn't worried by the fact that it had no prior experience in the field. Its affinity with its customers and its track record in other past ventures gave it credibility. Behind the scenes, Branson was savvy enough to partner with a major player that had both the operational experience and the capital to get the project off the ground. Deutsche Telecom took a 50 percent stake in the £170 million joint venture and provided the cellular backbone via its subsidiary, One-2-One. In one stroke, Virgin Mobile became the largest virtual mobile network operator in the world.

By the first quarter of 2002, the operation was running in the black, less than three years after it started. Subscribers numbered more than 1.5 million. The company is growing so fast that it already ranks as the fifth biggest cell phone network in the UK. In 2002, Virgin Mobile debuted in the U.S. market via a $300 million joint venture with Sprint PCS.

The company's results have been all the more remarkable given the slowing growth of the market as a whole. Branson notes, "We are particularly proud because we've done all this in a market that has seen mobile growth fall by a factor of five over the past year."

To the extent that Virgin's branding is unusually flexible and supported by its founder's iconic personality, it might seem that its story lacks relevance for other consumer companies. But almost every brand is capable of being built out along affinity lines to some extent. Consumer companies can emulate Virgin by asking themselves: In thinking about our brand and the meaning it has for our customers, how might we expand the brand beyond its functionality attributes to create more emotional connection to customers? In doing so, what new opportunities could we exploit?

Or turn the question around and focus on the Virgin Mobile opportunity. What other companies have hip and innovative brands that might have supported a move into this space? How about The Gap, MTV, Apple Computer, or Mountain Dew?

A strong brand is a wonderful thing, but a brand that speaks to a consumer's emotional need to feel part of a larger affinity group is like a universal key— it can unlock virtually any market.

Riding with the Pack

Many other brands have the emotional potency to allow their owners to pursue new-growth paths as Virgin has. Harley-Davidson markets a rich array of product and service offerings around the "rebels-of-the-open-road" image that its motorcycles connote. Nike has leveraged its connection with athletic achievement into a broader brand image that focuses on inspiration and self-expression. Starbucks has turned a commodity product, coffee, into a component of a branded lifestyle. Viacom has used its successful MTV and Nickelodeon franchises, which set teen and preteen trends, to move into record and film production, toys, books, and concert promotion. And even GM has been building its Hummer sport utility brand into a broader lifestyle offering.

Yet there are countless other brands with untapped reservoirs of customer affinity. Take Coke, for instance. Given its credibility as a refreshing beverage, the Coke name is easily extended to other soft drinks (as in the case of Diet Coke and Diet Coke with Lemon). Yet on an emotional level, Coke is much more than a beverage. It represents a quintessentially American lifestyle that embraces fun, family, and an energetic spirit. One can easily imagine the Coke brand being attached to new products and services on these terms.

Coke has chosen not to build out its brand, however beyond its minor foray into clothing and collectibles. Nor has McDonald's, another company whose brand is among the most recognized in the world. The McDonald's corporate identity is both clear and compelling, yet it has chosen not to stray outside its sizable niche in the fast-food arena.

Imagining the possibilities for major brands makes for an intriguing challenge. If Gillette moved beyond its product attributes (close, reliable shaving), it might expand into the emotional realm of male vanity, or even precision engineering. How about Kellogg? Moving beyond tastiness and nutrition, it could expand into healthfulness, vitality, or family togetherness.

The affinity approach does have its drawbacks. Where the brand position is weak (New Balance versus Nike) or focused heavily on product attributes (Toyota), attempts to forge a sense of community with consumers can prove difficult. In the summer of 2001, less than a year after committing to a $50 million joint venture mobile phone deal in Singapore, Virgin walked away from the deal, having managed to lure just fifty thousand customers. The Virgin brand just didn't have the same recognition or credibility in Singapore as in Britain.

An Image Problem

In some cases, the opportunity to reach out and connect with customers in new ways can be literal rather than symbolic. The Internet and other communications technologies make this possible in many situations where it was once too difficult or expensive.

Kodak, for instance, has taken advantage of digital technology to reach and serve customers in ways it never could before. By leveraging the hidden asset of its experience and credibility in the photographic field and jumping on the shift to digital photography, Kodak has been able to meet customers' next-generation needs for fast, inexpensive, high-quality, creative image management.

From its beginning, Kodak was built on the principle of bringing modern imaging technology to the people. Founder George Eastman mass-produced the first consumer cameras at the end of the nineteenth century. In recent years, however, Kodak has been plagued by a common problem among consumer companies: Because its products and services are distributed to the public primarily via third-party retailers, it has had little connection to its end users.

What's more, Kodak's customers didn't give much thought to the purchase transaction. Nobody lies awake at night worrying about where to buy a $5 roll of film or about what kind of film to purchase. Most people just want to snap a few shots on a holiday weekend and drop off the film at the one-hour processor the next morning. It appeared that Kodak's offering was one that presented few opportunities to add value.

Kodak, therefore, was poorly positioned to address customers' next-generation needs. And the company was suffering fundamental growth woes. By the 1980s, Agfa and Fujifilm were quickly eroding Kodak's share of the photographic film market. In the late 1990s, the increasing popularity of digital photography called into question the future prospects of the traditional film market. Between 1999 and 2001, Kodak's operating income in its main photography business declined by nearly a third.

Kodak needed a way to connect to its customers. The solution it turned to was the same new technology that was eroding its base business—digital media. By thinking creatively about the possibilities in digital images and the Internet, Kodak was able to forge a new connection to the consumer and at the same time to fundamentally alter the nature of the product purchase from a low-cost, low-emotional-involvement transaction to one involving a rich array of tailored services and support.

By 2001, Americans owned nearly fifteen million digital cameras. But most needed help with this new technology, which represented the first major change in photography in a century. If used to its full potential, it could allow new flexibility in processing, editing, sharing, archiving, and displaying photos. Kodak's research showed that 17 percent of all Internet users had already used online services to store photos, and 27 percent of these had ordered prints online. How could the company step into this new game?

On a Roll

Kodak made its move in 2001 by purchasing Ofoto, a one-year-old Berkeley, Calif.-based online image processing firm. Ofoto's mission: to give photographers a new and easier way to store and share pictures online, and to provide top-quality silver halide prints for both digital and film camera users. In outline, Ofoto's proposition is similar to that of its competitors. Digital customers upload their images directly to the website, where they can be stored, processed, and archived using free proprietary software. Users of traditional film can do the same by mailing in their film and paying a $3.95 fee per roll. CD-ROM discs containing all the photos in an archive are available for $10 each, while high-quality prints are sold for $.50 to $20 each, depending on the size.

The Ofoto service lets customers selectively order prints of their favorite photos. It lets them share the images with distant family and friends by allowing users to create virtual albums on the Ofoto site. It lets them archive their electronic images cheaply and easily. It lets them mount the photos in customized picture frames and personalized cards. And, on a higher level, it saves time, improves quality, and reduces the complexity of the photographic experience. From selling one piece of the imaging process—the film—Kodak is now able to sell the entire process and auxiliary goods and services as well.

Kodak brings to Ofoto several significant advantages over its start-up competitors: decades of experience in mass-market image processing, a brand name virtually synonymous with photography, and substantial marketing clout.

As a result, Ofoto has grown quickly under the Kodak banner. The new customer base is growing at 12 percent per month, and average revenues per transaction have increased by 31 percent since 2000. In 2002, Ofoto hopes to achieve $60 million in sales. Not bad for a fledgling unit, but miniscule compared to the industry's future potential. By 2005, Americans will have bought more than forty million digital cameras and will be spending more than $1 billion a year on digital photo services. If it continues to evolve its business model, Ofoto (which is now the second largest digital photography site on the Web) can expect to capture a sizable chunk of that market.

For Kodak, Ofoto represents an opportunity beyond additional revenue. The service will allow Kodak to form a direct relationship with consumers, making it possible to market new services and products to end users, gather information about them, and develop new offers to serve their broader image-related needs.

Not every consumer company stands to benefit from advances in information technology. You can't digitize a turkey sandwich or deliver lawn furniture through fiber-optic cable. But this is not an isolated phenomenon or opportunity.

Across a wide range of consumer industries, more and more companies are wrapping information and customization around many kinds of purchases. It is happening in music, where file-swapping services add archiving, sharing, and chat; in banking, where online banking provides asset management and bill-paying convenience; and in video rentals, where Netflix has added recommendations, online ordering, and a queue of ready-to-send movies to the traditional rental service. All are significantly improving the customer's purchase and ownership experience by tapping developments in the Internet and related technologies.

Unfortunately, established companies are rarely at the forefront of these consumer enhancements. On the contrary—as in the case of the music industry, they are often leading the efforts to thwart such changes.

Kodak's success story offers a valuable lesson. Creative thinking can uncover previously unrecognized ways to reach out and touch the customer. It may be by exploiting a new technology, by developing a new distribution channel, or by working in new ways with the existing channels.

Branching Out

Sometimes there aren't any obvious opportunities to serve the customer in new ways that lead to growth. The brand may not resonate on an emotional level. Internet or not, there may be little valuable additional interaction or information to deliver. When this is the case, the best way of opening up new paths of growth may be to step back and rethink the definition of the customer. Kraft and Fidelity are two companies pursuing this approach—Kraft by providing a sophisticated category management service to grocery chains, Fidelity by developing a suite of back-office services and tools that help financial advisers run the administration and analysis parts of their businesses. A third company is Intuit, the maker of consumer financial management software.

In the late 1990s, Intuit's flagship products—Quicken, TurboTax, and Quickbooks—had reached the boundaries of traditional growth. The three software titles so dominated their respective markets that they had nowhere to grow. Intuit's personal tax preparation software had already captured 71 percent revenue share in its market, its personal financial management software 78 percent, and its small-business software 85 percent.

Intuit saw the potential to extend these software positions into seamless bill paying, portfolio management, and financial transaction management for consumers through an online financial portal. But its efforts were stymied by the banks and brokerage firms that controlled such information, and consumers' reluctance to trust a monolithic financial gatekeeper. When the Internet bubble collapsed in 2001, Intuit's last hopes for growing in this direction were left in tatters.

Under the leadership of a new CEO, Intuit decided to move in a bold new direction. Instead of deepening its connection to its core customer base, it would redefine its offering to shift its focus toward what had previously been a peripheral market: small to medium-sized businesses.

In the past, Intuit had pursued only small businesses with fewer than twenty employees. Now, leveraging the asset of expertise in the financial software field, Intuit was able to aggressively move into a new market, companies with between 20 and 250 employees.

Compared to individual consumers, small businesses have much more complex financial needs, which are often tightly intertwined with their operational functions and issues. For Intuit, this meant many more complex, mission-critical needs it could address. Small businesses represent a huge potential market for payroll and HR/benefits software and for vertical business management software that can help take care of everything from inventory control to customer tracking. For instance, software designed for a property management company could run lease tracking, property information, tenant data, wait-list tracking, rent control, move-in/out processing, and accounting. All in all, the total opportunity in selling management software to small to medium-sized businesses is worth more than $18 billion.

Furthermore, this market is less variable than Intuit's traditional market. A hugely disproportionate share of Intuit's sales has traditionally come in the first quarter of the year, during income tax season. The broader business software market offers year-round opportunities.

In search of the skills and software needed to play in these new areas, Intuit has acquired a number of specialized business software providers and revamped its sales force. Though the company's new strategy is still in the rollout stage, preliminary results are encouraging. Intuit's revenue and margins have been growing despite a disastrous overall software market. The company's pretax operating margins are now more than 20 percent, compared to 13 percent the year before Intuit began its shift in focus.

The Big Picture

Throughout the consumer space, increasing competition and diminishing differentiation are making growth harder and harder to come by. But no matter what the sector, there are always customers with new and unmet needs experiencing frustrations, unnecessary costs, delays, and aggravation. Finding those customers and figuring out how to solve their problems is the key to future growth.

As we have seen, there's a wide variety of creative ways to translate next-generation consumer needs into new growth and competitive differentiation. If you are part of a company trying to escape the growth doldrums, you might want to borrow from the playbooks of the growth exemplars we have profiled by asking the following questions:

- What does the broader ownership or consumption process surrounding your product or service look like? Where are there consumer points of pain or anxiety that you might help address?
- Could your brand resonate with consumers on an emotional level? Could the brand serve as an affinity hub through which consumers can fulfill their need for belonging? When you think about it from that perspective, could it allow you to play in interesting new markets? Are there things you can do to begin to evolve your brand in this direction?
- Are there creative new ways to reach out and interact with your customers more intimately and cost-effectively than in the past? If so, what new offerings might be enabled by these new connections?
- Step back and examine your business landscape from afar. Are there elements on the periphery of

your core market—untapped customer sets or sales channels, for instance—that might represent fruitful opportunities for growth through serving next-generation needs?

15

Information Everywhere: Tsutaya, Dassault Systemes, and GE Medical Systems

Sleeping Giant

In 2001, for the first time in history, U.S. investment in information technology surpassed spending on traditional plant and equipment. For most companies, information is becoming the largest asset that they own. And information assets are only growing more pervasive. People continue to digitize new forms of content ranging from X rays to movies, and to develop smaller and more mobile information tools such as wearable computers. Information can increasingly reach customers almost anywhere in precisely the format they prefer, thereby enlarging the value and flexibility of information-based offerings.

This is good news for next-generation growth because information assets possess several attractive characteristics from a demand innovation perspective. First, they are particularly powerful for addressing complex customer needs such as managing risk and uncertainty, improving work flows, and anticipating rather than responding to problems. In each of these cases, timely, accurate information is critical.

Second, information assets are among the most reusable assets. Information systems, for example, are expensive and time-consuming to deploy, but once the software has been written and the information has been captured, it can be reused at very low marginal cost. A final attractive characteristic of information is that it can be customized and delivered remotely to customers very quickly and at a low cost.

Thus, information is emerging as a critical category of hidden asset. Most of the demand innovators we have profiled are evolving new businesses based on leveraging their information assets.

Yet many companies have tapped only a tiny portion of their information's potential for driving new growth. Why is that?

One reason is that managers often don't recognize the wealth of information assets they own. They tend to think in terms of traditional information assets like computer systems, customer relationship management databases, and little more. In fact, information assets actually encompass a broad range of data and data management tools. Valuable assets that are often overlooked include warranty information, transaction histories, technical expertise, research results, point-of-sale data, equipment monitoring software and data, and a host of custom analytic tools that individuals throughout the firm have built to help them do their jobs better.

In addition, since the bursting of the dot-com bubble, some managers tend to disparage ideas that involve digital assets, rolling their eyes at anything that resembles an "e-business" or "digital initiative." But a thoughtless rejection of digital business is just as expensive as the thoughtless enthusiasm many businesses fell prey to in the late 1990s.

So how can you use information assets to drive new growth? The examples of three companies—Tsutaya, Dassault Systemes, and GE Medical Systems—can help start your thinking about how to uncover and use your own information assets.

Tsutaya: Using Customer Information to Boost Sales and Create New Revenue Streams

Think of your local Blockbuster video store. Now think of an insightful Blockbuster on steroids crossed with the local Borders book and music store and you get a sense of how Tsutaya has taken Japan by storm.

Founded in 1985, Tsutaya has evolved from a small retailer with unexceptional growth into the leading renter of videos in Japan, with $650 million in revenues, eleven hundred superstores, and a 31 percent market share. It has also become one of the top retailers for music and books, categories in which it ranks second and seventh, respectively, in sales. Tsutaya accomplished this by using its customer data assets to drive marketing and sales efforts, tailor customer offerings, and create information packages for sale to other companies.

From the start, Tsutaya devoted a lot of resources to collecting customer data and figuring out how the data could both provide value to customers and improve company performance. By the early 1990s, the company had built comprehensive customer profiles from point-of-sale data, responses to customer questionnaires, sampling, and direct marketing. As its database grew, Tsutaya's knowledge became more precise, moving from general analysis of sales trends to insights into the behavior of individual customers.

Initially, Tsutaya used customer data much as other sophisticated retailers do to improve its demand forecasting, which allowed stores to increase sales in certain areas and to reduce the level of unsold inventory. This was a valuable first step, but Tsutaya had more ambitious plans. In 1999, the company launched Tsutaya Online (TOL), a website that keeps consumers posted on the latest entertainment news while serving as a powerful communication channel between Tsutaya and its customers. Today, TOL is the most popular entertainment site in Japan, with 2.6 million members and more than fifty million page views per month.

The combination of Tsutaya's rich customer data and TOL has created a mutually reinforcing system that, like many information networks, becomes more potent the more it is used. Tsutaya captures data about customer preferences from every customer interaction in the store or on the Internet. Each time someone chooses a specific e-magazine or responds to a coupon offer, the company understands that person's interests a little bit more. As Tsutaya's understanding of customers grows, it can craft more closely tailored offerings and recommendations, which generate more interactions, more sales, and more data, allowing the company to refine its offerings even further.

Consider how Tsutaya uses this information and insight to interact with a twenty-eight-year-old Tokyo salaryman we will call Yuji Nishino. Yuji is a fan of the band Dragon Ash, as noted in Tsutaya's database. Yuji bought the group's last three albums from Tsutaya and downloaded a schedule of Dragon Ash's recent concert tour from TOL.

One day, while riding the train from work to his suburban apartment, Yuji checks e-mail from his mobile phone. One message is a reminder from Tsutaya about the upcoming release of Dragon Ash's brand-new album, including the title, release date, reviews, and an option to reserve a copy at his local Tsutaya store. That's convenient, because the album will likely sell out quickly, and Yuji will be in Kyoto on business next week. By using his phone to reserve his copy ahead of time, he will have the CD to enjoy over the weekend after returning from Kyoto.

A week later, as he drives to the Tsutaya store to pick up the album, his wife, Fumiko, calls him on the cell phone and asks him to pick up the new *Star Wars* movie on DVD. While en route, he uses the phone to check Tsutaya's inventory. He sees that there are only two copies remaining at the local branch, so he makes a reservation request via phone. Arriving at the store, Yuji recalls an article that TOL had sent him about a new musician that many Dragon Ash fans are excited about. He finds that artist's debut album and buys it along with his two reserved items. Total time in the store: ten minutes.

Tsutaya's ability to capture and synthesize patterns of behavior in order to tailor offers to individual consumers via the Web clearly helps people make better decisions in less time. For Tsutaya, it translates directly into improved performance and value creation. No more buying costly inventory of CDs, DVDs, or books based on a merchandiser's hunch; Tsutaya has hard data about customer preferences that guide smarter purchasing decisions, thereby improving the ratio of sales to invested capital, reducing out-of-stock problems, and minimizing expensive return shipments of goods to manufacturers.

Tsutaya reaps other benefits as well. Tsutaya Online customers visit stores 22 percent more often than non–TOL members and spend an average of 9 percent more. And the bond between company and customers continues to deepen. Between 1996 and 2001, Tsutaya's annual revenue per member increased from $11 to $49, and its revenue per store increased from $125,000 to $757,000, fueling an overall revenue growth rate of 49 percent. Profit margins have also increased over the past five years. Since going public in the second quarter of 2000, Tsutaya's stock price has increased at a compound annual growth rate of 34 percent, while the Nikkei 225 index has averaged a 22 percent annual loss.

Tsutaya's use of information assets to enhance the performance of its core business is impressive. These assets can also become the basis of an entirely new business.

Tsutaya's customer database, which tracks more than sixteen million customers and two to three million pieces of point-of-sale data daily, has become a huge information asset whose full value can't be mined by Tsutaya alone. Through a sister company, ADMS, Tsutaya now sells data and analytical support to companies developing marketing plans, new products, and sales promotions. Clients include companies such as beer maker Kirin, which is eager to gain the customer insight it needs to fine-tune its marketing plans. Though this business is still relatively small, with $27 million in revenues in 2001, it is growing at a double-digit rate.

Tsutaya's success is even more striking when compared to industry peers such as SHICHIE, Kotobuki Industry, and Towa Meccs, which have stagnated or experienced significant declines in sales in recent years. The difference, says Muneaki Masuda, Tsutaya's CEO: "We're not interested in merely renting videos to people. We're collecting lifestyle information, and the possibilities that flow from that are, over time, enormous."

Dassault Systemes: Packaging Internal Software for External Customers

Avions Marcel Dassault, one of Europe's leading aeronautical firms, ran into a significant problem back in the 1970s, when digital tools were still in their infancy. In 1975, Dassault had purchased a CADAM (Computer Aided Drafting and Manufacturing) software license from Lockheed. The deal made Dassault one of the world's first CADAM customers. But Dassault soon discovered that Lockheed's two-dimensional software wasn't sophisticated enough for use in designing France's Mirage fighter jet. Seeing no other options on the market, Dassault decided to create its own three-dimensional software, called CATIA.

It soon became apparent to Dassault that its CATIA software was better than any existing package and that it would be valuable to other companies as well. To pursue this opportunity, Dassault decided to create a separate company, Dassault Systemes. Although Dassault would retain a 51 percent ownership share and play an active role in the new company's development, being independent would allow Systemes to focus on commercializing CATIA rather than on supporting Dassault's engineers. At the same time, the connection to Dassault would help Systemes in several important ways. It gave Systemes instant credibility with very demanding aerospace customers. It provided a beta testing laboratory for new software products. And it introduced Systemes staff to Dassault's partners in various aerospace programs.

However, it took much more to build Systemes into a successful business. Dassault quickly recognized that Systemes lacked a large-scale sales force and extensive contacts in industries outside of aerospace. So early on, Systemes formed an alliance with IBM, which agreed to market CATIA in return for a share of the profits. Systemes thus gained access to IBM's global sales force, which had customer relationships in virtually every industry. This relationship has proven beneficial to both parties and remains in effect to this day.

Starting from its expertise in the aerospace industry, Systemes gradually broadened into new industries, simultaneously increasing the ability of its software to address the higher-order needs of customers. Over time, Systemes has greatly increased the functionality of its products while extending itself along the design and manufacturing spectrum. Originally focused on drafting, Systemes expanded its product line to support design, analysis, simulation, engineering, and production. Systemes now helps customers with every stage of a manufacturing process, from design to digital testing for design flaws through manufacturing and quality control. Customers can even collaborate on projects with suppliers and partners, further improving and streamlining complex design and manufacturing projects.

As a result, Systemes software has wide appeal. It not only offers greater design capabilities but also helps shorten time to market, reduces risks and costs, and increases product reliability. Today, CATIA software is used to design and manufacture products ranging from automobiles to naval yards to lingerie, by customers including Formula One, Goodyear, Bang & Olufsen, Boeing, and Shell.

By understanding its customers' processes and addressing their top priorities, Systemes has achieved 22 percent market share with profit margins of 30 percent, double those of its nearest competitor and almost six times the industry average. The company went public in 1996 and is now the number two software company in Europe, generating more than $600 million in revenues.

Dassault's experience illustrates how an internally developed system can be transformed from a basic tool and expense of the core business into a tremendous new-growth platform even more valuable than the core business. As of July 2002, despite the collapse of technology markets, Systemes had a market capitalization of $5.2 billion, compared to Dassault's $3.5 billion. Not bad for a company that started with three employees from Dassault's information systems department.

Other companies have captured external value from commercializing their internal information systems. For instance, Sabre was an information system designed by American Airlines to handle travel reservations for itself and later for other airlines as well. Ultimately spun off as a separate company, Sabre's market value in July 2002 stood at $3.3 billion while its former parent, AMR, had a market capitalization of just $1.6 billion.

In another example, Kansas City Southern Railroad took a data processing system created to manage its own operations and transformed it into the leading system for processing mutual fund transactions—DST Systems.

Many other companies have also created internal

capabilities with extraordinary potential to create new growth—a potential still waiting to be tapped.

GE Medical Systems: Capitalizing on By-Product Information

GE faces a unique challenge. As an early pioneer of demand innovation, it has created a decade of growth from pursuing financing and service opportunities that grew from its core product sales. But now GE is a services behemoth, with some $60 billion in nonproduct sales. Finding the next platform for growth is, therefore, a high priority.

One of the primary places GE is looking for its next big growth opportunity is in putting its information assets to work. GE Medical Systems (GEMS) is a good example.

In 1995, GEMS was a $4 billion division of General Electric that sold medical imaging equipment to hospitals. Today, it is an $8.5 billion company comprising three business segments—healthcare services, imaging equipment, and information technology—that improves the flow of all sorts of clinical and administrative information across hospital networks, and is positioned to revolutionize how hospitals manage information and make decisions.

The transformation of GEMS is a by-product of the shift from analog to digital imaging and the company's realization that the information created by its equipment was the key to addressing many of the most pressing priorities that hospitals face.

The equipment that GEMS sells, such as X-ray machines, magnetic resonance imaging equipment, and computer tomography scanners, creates critical information that hospitals rely on to deliver high-quality medical care: the X ray of a broken leg, the results from a cardiac stress test, or the ultrasound image of a fetus. Such images set in motion a whole series of procedures and are referred to again and again by a variety of medical professionals.

Starting in the mid-1990s, medical images that traditionally had been produced on film began to be captured in digital format. Suddenly, GEMS was positioned to help hospitals store, analyze, and communicate this information more efficiently. As a result, radiology departments could be run more efficiently with less paper and administrative hassles. More important, care might be improved without increasing costs. Doctors and nurses could have more timely and accurate information while collaborating with their colleagues more easily, hospital work processes could be streamlined, and patients could benefit from faster decision making and less duplication of tests.

GEMS's first move toward realizing this vision was to develop a Picture Archiving and Communication System (PACS). This is a network that stores the images created by medical imaging equipment in digital form, allowing medical staff to view the images on computer screens or print them out. PACS also stores diagnostic notes and records related to each image and can capture all the images associated with an individual patient in a single file. Thus, instead of searching for paper records, a doctor can quickly access all the information related to a particular case.

Moreover, the network allows several doctors in different locations to access a particular image at the same time, making it easier to collaborate on diagnoses. And PACS now includes software to help doctors evaluate the images they are looking at—for example, by highlighting the differences between a current magnetic resonance image of a patient and one that was taken a month ago.

For GEMS, this system created a lucrative new market in software, systems design, and ongoing support services. For hospitals, it's a way to achieve a tangible, positive return on their information technology in investments, with concrete benefits to patients.

Cheryl Martin, director of radiology for the Henry Ford Hospital in Detroit, told us about one way that PACS improves patient care. Before PACS, a patient might visit a satellite care facility on a Friday afternoon to have an injured arm X-rayed. Factoring in the availability of specialists at the satellite location and the need to print the X ray and send it by van to the main hospital, it might be as late as noon on Monday before the referring physician received a report from radiology with the definitive results of the X ray.

With PACS, even if there is no specialist at the satellite facility, the image can be viewed by a radiologist on call at the main hospital and the patient can receive care immediately. "Not only is there less hassle for the patients, but we also deliver better results," Martin said.

PACS opened up a major new opportunity for GEMS, but it was just a first step into improving the quagmire of hospital administration and information systems.

To be able to tie radiology information into broader hospital systems, GEMS launched a series of capability acquisitions, including Applicare Medical Imaging, ProAct Medical, VitalCom, and iPath. These acquisitions added capabilities such as monitoring patient data through a wireless network, integrating data from various departments of a hospital, and benchmarking operational performance. GEMS has also acquired middleware expertise to link its new offerings to hospitals' legacy systems, positioning itself to credibly pursue the goal of seamless healthcare information integration one department at a time.

GEMS is now able to improve the flow of both clinical and administrative information across the entire hospital network. Administrators can monitor patients remotely, electronically transfer a patient's medical history to a satellite clinic or a doctor's home, and optimize the use of operating rooms through improved scheduling. Although few hospitals have yet to adopt fully digitized, institutionwide IT systems, they are moving steadily in this direction as administrators and doctors realize the value such systems provide.

As with many successful new growth strategies, GEMS's moves have led to a situation in which everyone benefits. Patients receive better treatment; doctors and other professionals make better decisions while saving time and energy; and hospitals can control costs, work more efficiently, and avoid malpractice suits. Reflecting on the implementation of PACS to help her manage the six hundred thousand radiology studies conducted annually at her hospital, Martin told us: "I can't add cost, and I can't add people. I need to work smarter. PACS is helping me do this."

Meanwhile, GEMS has more than quadrupled the size of its addressable market, expanding from the market for radiology equipment into hospital IT and now into overall hospital administration. The Information Technology division is expected to outpace other divisions of GEMS, with annual growth of 20 to 30 percent per year.

From an initial position as an established provider of high-quality imaging equipment, GEMS has repositioned itself as a critical economic partner for hospitals and other health providers. Moving beyond the initial targets of reducing costs and improving the efficiency of basic operations, GEMS is now positioned to transform information flows and decision making throughout hospital systems—all a result of recognizing the relevance of its by-product information to the next-generation needs of its customers.

Can You Turn Information into Profit Growth?

As the stories of Tsutaya, Dassault Systemes, and GE Medical Systems suggest, there are many ways that information assets can create significant new value and new growth. They can help maximize product sales and support premium pricing; they can be sold directly, in such forms as by-product information, software systems, and services; and they can be the basis of entirely new businesses, such as performance guarantees, risk management programs, and market making.

Is information-driven growth a promising path for your company? The following questions will help you evaluate the opportunities:

- Which information assets do you own? Which ones will you develop over the next three years?
- Do you generate by-product information in your core business that might have value for either your current customers or a new set of customers? What customer data do you collect that you are not using or underusing?
- How good are the custom information systems you've created for managing your own business? Who else within and outside your industry might want to use them?
- Are elements of your offering or your output becoming digital? What new-growth opportunities does that represent?

Most companies are only just beginning to realize the relevance and growth potential of their information assets. Exploring and developing the value of your information assets today will give you a head start on your competitors.

PART FIVE

Getting Started

16

Some Moves for
Monday Morning

What Can We Do Right Away?

Setting a company on the course for growth by using hidden assets doesn't happen overnight. Most established businesses have trained themselves well in product-centric and R&D-based thinking. But they have not invested to fully develop their abilities in the field of demand innovation. Thus, when it comes to analyzing customers to discover their priorities, building new buyer relationships, and turning new opportunities into real profit, many companies have yet to build the systemic capabilities required.

Yet most companies are also under immediate pressure to improve their growth prospects. The focus of investors, especially the big institutions that hold so much power on Wall Street, is notoriously short-term.

So what can you do now, based on your current book of business, to jump-start your new-growth capabilities and improve your bottom line over the next few quarters?

This is where short-term moves come in—practical and tactical ideas you can start implementing immediately, built on your current business. This chapter offers a collection of some of the most effective short-term moves, which can generate quick gains in revenue and profits and also can launch your company on the process of developing the new mind-set, capabilities and instincts you'll need for creating long-term growth.

The Magnificent Seven

A variety of short-term moves represent *transitional* sources of profits and skills. All involve viewing and serving your customer in creative ways, using resources currently at hand. Some of the most valuable moves include:

1. **Deaveraging and resegmenting the customer base.** Many companies can enjoy significant short-term gains just by taking a fresh look at their traditional customer base through the lens of next-generation needs. Customers who appear monolithic in behavior when viewed through traditional segmentation prisms such as demographics may have very different next-generation needs. For instance, OnStar has identified new opportunities for growth by recognizing that road war-

riors like traveling salesmen and executives have different service needs than the average OnStar customer. Addressing unique needs can drive high-margin incremental revenue to the business while building valuable new customer insight.

2. **Building a strategic customer relationship program** to begin forging relationships deeper in the customer's organization can jump-start new growth, while also enhancing one's ability to observe and respond to the customer. For example, consider how Clarke American's key account program allowed it to develop new services for its financial institution partners. A successful strategic customer program can help minimize price-based competition while increasing a company's share of the customer's spending.

3. **Replicating the best customer relationship.** In most companies, innovative partnering and value-capture relationships exist with a special customer or two, sometimes known only to a handful of field sales or technical support people. Often, tremendous value can be unlocked by identifying and replicating such relationships with other valuable customers. A good example of this was Johnson Controls' ability to leverage the unique aspects of its relationships with Chrysler into a new way of doing business with other automakers.

4. **Value pricing** can be another powerful boost for short-term profits. Value pricing approaches include breaking an all-inclusive price into its component parts and charging for valuable but formerly "free" add-on services—a tack that air-

lines, credit card providers, and others are taking. Another approach involves developing the ability to demonstrate to customers the tangible value that you create for them as a means of influencing price negotiations in your favor.

5. **Evolving the product offer into a system offer.** Many product and service providers have discovered that they can boost revenues per customer and profits by turning their stand-alone product into one component of a system of products designed to work together. Ensure, the nutritional supplement brand, does this by offering an integrated suite of nutritional drinks and foods that work together to provide balanced nutrition. Applied Materials and Apple Computer have built a system offer by designing a suite of hardware offerings configured to work best when wired to each other.

6. **Putting a value-added wrapper around the product offering.** In many cases, you can quickly address next-generation needs and increase your product differentiation by wrapping easy-to-deliver but valuable supporting services around the product. UPS has done this with its tracking services and BMW by incorporating regular maintenance and roadside assistance into the price of its vehicles.

7. **Shifting the brand equity investments to emphasize the emotional and affinity elements of the brand.** Even the most product-oriented brands typically resonate with customers on some softer dimensions. Companies often find that they can boost brand awareness and loyalty, while also building credibility for future forays into next-

generation needs, by emphasizing these elements. A good example is a consumer lending company that found it had underexploited equity in the customers' view of it as an easy and friendly company with which to do business. Communicating this element of its brand equity led to increased differentiation and higher share in a crowded market.

Many of these short-term moves can be driven by middle managers without waiting for approval and funding from senior management. As we've seen, middle managers are uniquely placed to develop new-growth strategies for their companies. They own much of the information residing in the organizational knowledge bank, are close to customers, and have a network of colleagues with whom they can collaborate on projects below the corporate radar. These moves are relatively simple to launch from the middle levels of the organization, without creating bureaucracies that suck up organizational energy.

Short-Term Moves in Action

Home Depot: Resegmenting the Customer Base in Search of Quick Growth Hits

Home Depot dominates the home improvement category, offering a full range of hardware, building, and decor products in its big-box retail format. Its stores carry virtually the same assortment of products in generally the same layout.

Home Depot's original vision was to serve the do-it-yourself consumer, yet the stores actually serve customers with a wide variety of needs, ranging from guys picking up supplies for a weekend porch-building project and couples looking for a new light fixture for the bathroom to the occasional home remodeling contractor.

But serving these different segments and actually catering to their unique needs are two very different things. While Home Depot's broad concept has brought a diverse set of customers in the door, it wasn't really satisfying all of them. This wasn't a priority issue until the late 1990s, when Home Depot began to run out of places to build new stores, leading to the first real growth crisis in the company's history.

The need to focus more urgently on growth led Home Depot to examine its customer base more closely. Two underserved customer categories stood out: women shoppers doing decor projects, and contractors.

To address the decor project opportunity, Home Depot has created the Expo store concept (as we discussed in chapter 3). Contractors were another story, and one with even greater immediate significance. They represent a huge portion of the market for home improvement products and services, but they didn't shop much at Home Depot. If the company could pick up a larger share of the contractor market through its traditional stores, it would quickly boost same-store sales and profits.

When Home Depot examined contractors to understand how they might be different from the average customer, it discovered that contractors typically shop more frequently, buy in larger quantities, and have a high volume of repeat purchases. This meant that the inconvenience of navigating the big store and waiting in line for checkout weighed more heavily on them than on the homeowner customer. They also tend to shop early in the morning to prepare for a day on the job site, and they use short-term credit heavily to cope with uncertain cash flow.

Home Depot is now addressing these and other important contractor issues through its new Pro Initiative offering, which provides enhanced services and merchandise. Contractors can phone in orders and have the goods ready and waiting for them when they arrive at the store; they can qualify for bulk discounts and new revolving credit programs; and they can take advantage of such special customized services as tool rental, a set-aside checkout area, and help with truck loading and deliveries. Providing these services requires only modest modifications to the Home Depot store layout and limited additional employee training.

In a recent twist, Home Depot has begun to experiment with adding Dunkin' Donuts outlets to their stores, attempting to make Home Depot *the* stop for contractors in the morning. The 220-square-foot outlets have seating with Internet hookups and serve the full range of Dunkin' Donut offerings, including hot and cold beverages, baked goods, and breakfast sandwiches. It's a clever way of catering to customers who were going to go to Dunkin' Donuts anyway and now can do so at their leisure, as they are having their trucks loaded with the lumber, plumbing parts, and tools they need for the day.

So far, close to two-thirds of Home Depot's four-teen hundred stores have incorporated the Pro Initiative offerings, and their sales per square foot are already 12 percent higher than in the average Home Depot store. Given the high fixed costs of running a store, this represents a disproportionate growth in store profitability. Thus, the company can probably count on the Pro Initiative for several more quarters of profit gain as the program is rolled out to other stores. And the lucrative contractor segment is now the fastest-growing one at Home Depot, having grown to constitute 30 percent of its customer base.

The Pro Initiative has helped set the stage for new long-term growth as well. By developing a much stronger relationship with this valuable customer segment, Home Depot may be able to work with contractors to jointly offer services for projects that are too large for the average do-it-yourselfer.

WorldWire Telecom: Replicating the Best Customer Relationships

At a global company that we'll call "WorldWire," a few enterprising salespeople were in the habit of providing special "sweeteners," ad hoc supporting services, in order to nail down multimillion-dollar telecommunications contracts with large corporate customers. Typically, this involved cajoling the engineers in network operations to provide customers with network monitoring tools and data that they could access directly.

One example is a direct link between the customer's telecom networking department and World-Wire's internal fault reporting and tracking systems. Traditionally, when a customer's network goes down, it must contact WorldWire, report the outage, and call repeatedly for progress reports. Providing a direct link for select customers reduced the frustration level and saved both sides time and money.

Another service focused on network monitoring and load reporting. WorldWire has sophisticated systems that immediately report developing problems such as traffic congestion on a particular part of the network. For select customers, WorldWire began providing direct access into WorldWire's system, letting clients more effectively manage their own network usage patterns.

These and other special services had been created without formal direction or corporate support from above. The account managers used funds from general account support budgets. In fact, WorldWire's senior managers might never even have heard of these various programs if they hadn't been uncovered in a survey of corporate e-initiatives.

When senior managers began to understand the popularity of these add-on services, a larger idea emerged. Why not create an integrated collection of the special services that could be *sold* to customers, transforming them into a systematic and more profitable offering?

The result was a set of customizable extranet templates dubbed Service Circles. They let individual customers review performance statistics, access fault archives, look at bills, study blueprint documents, and access network monitoring systems, all without having to engage the help of a WorldWire expert.

The pricing of Service Circles varies by the size and complexity of the customer. A bare-bones version is generally available for little or no extra charge, but any bells and whistles cost extra. For example, a $6-million-a-year networking contract might generate an extra $500,000 in Service Circle upgrades— revenue that is highly profitable, since the cost of developing the system has already been absorbed by WorldWire.

Some two hundred WorldWire customers now participate in Service Circles. They've given it many accolades, calling it "a fantastic source of information" and "unique in the industry." Over the past year, WorldWire's midlevel enterprise division has enjoyed an overall revenue increase of 10 percent, partly as a result of this initiative. More important, the experience has helped WorldWire expand its thinking about customer needs and the economic spaces surrounding their products.

ABC Risk: Using Value Pricing to Capture a Greater Share of the Customer Benefits Delivered

Commercial insurance brokers, including a company we will call ABC Risk, consult on and help their clients structure coverage programs for things such as catastrophic liability and executive liability. They are under increasing pricing pressure from clients to reduce their fees and to move away from the traditional commission system, where revenues rise with the value of the insurance placed, toward a flat-fee-based structure.

On the surface, this may seem a minor change. But because fee-based arrangements are no longer tied clearly to the value of the insurance, it has become imperative for brokers to find a way to successfully articulate and defend the value they deliver to clients. This transition led insurance companies in general, and ABC Risk in particular, to reexamine their pricing procedures. ABC had to find a way to be compensated for the increasing range of value-added services it had been offering, such as risk assessment and structuring, crisis management, and claims management and preparation.

To make this possible, ABC has developed a set of analytic and decision-making tools as part of account planning and contract negotiation to help its client managers be more effective at selling and pricing value-added services. These tools are based on the best practices discovered through a set of interviews with some of ABC's top sales executives, and they codify those practices in a form any skilled salesperson can master. They include a framework for evaluating the importance the client places on risk management, a questionnaire for evaluating and ranking services that the client might find valuable, and a template for articulating and quantifying the total value added that the company provides.

The goal is to help client managers focus their efforts on those accounts that most value the enhanced services and then be able to explain and defend the value that ABC Risk delivers.

The new tools are supported by training seminars and regular account team meetings. For example, each client now undergoes a services review by a committee of top-flight sales managers and experts in specific insurance product lines, to review the scope of services and advise salespeople on pricing issues. It's a way of ensuring that the best practices of the company are rapidly disseminated and implemented throughout the organization.

For some sales executives, the new tools have come as a revelation. Working through the process opens their eyes to a new way of approaching pricing and the entire client relationship. And even the most sophisticated and successful salespeople who already understood the fundamental premises of value pricing are pleased with the systematic process the new tools provide.

In one case, ABC had a long-standing client (call it "Smith Brothers Manufacturing") that had been generating some $550,000 in annual commissions.

The notion of shifting this client to value pricing made staffers nervous: "Why rock the boat?" they asked. "Smith has been with us for years, and it's set in its ways. Let's just stick with the status quo."

The new tools and the approach they encouraged made the difference. In preparation for a discussion with Smith Brothers, the ABC executive asked everyone on the service team, "Tell me three things you do that the Smith people value." With a little coaching, the team members produced a long list of special services they had been providing to Smith.

At the first contract renewal meeting, the ABC executive reviewed the list with Smith's risk manager, who was surprised to learn about all these services. When ABC then suggested that a more appropriate annual fee would be $1.2 million, the manager readily agreed, but pointed out that he couldn't justify such a large one-year increase to the top executives at Smith. The two settled on a compromise fee of $875,000 . . . a nearly 60 percent increase in ABC's compensation.

The new approach to pricing has done more than just enhance ABC Risk's bottom line. It has also strengthened customer relationships, an invaluable asset that will be leveraged in subsequent higher-order growth moves. More important, perhaps, ABC's sales force has begun to think more broadly about its customers' economics and to examine their own business through the same lens, thinking continually about new ways to deliver value to their clients and capture value in the process.

Applying Short-Term Tactics to Your Business

Although many short-term moves generate disproportionate benefits in terms of incremental revenues
and profits, don't judge them merely by the dollars
they generate directly. Their greater value lies in the
opportunity they create for learning about the customer and developing new capabilities. Today's
$1 million move may become the essential building
block that enables tomorrow's $100 million new-
growth business.

What opportunities are there to start your organization on the road to demand innovation? Ask yourself the following questions:

- Would looking at your customers through a be-
  havioral or economic lens suggest untapped opportunities for quick growth?
- Do you touch the customer through many different product divisions or at different levels? Could
  you benefit from a more coordinated approach to
  customer management?
- What do your best customer relationships look
  like? Do any of them suggest opportunities and relationships that could be adopted more widely?
- How closely does your pricing match the value
  you deliver? What opportunities are there to
  charge more or to unbundle your offering?

17

Creating Your
Growth Action Plan

In this book, we've highlighted next-generation growth opportunities, identified some of the challenges associated with seizing those opportunities, and discussed shorter-term activities and strategies that you can use to begin applying customer-centric thinking about higher-order needs at your company. But there are some questions we haven't yet tackled: How critical is growth to your company? And how can you focus on new growth in an integrated way and with the right level of intensity?

You probably need to start focusing on finding sources of new growth sooner than you think. The purpose of this chapter is to help you do that.

Where Is My Company on the Growth Curve?

In terms of their current growth needs, most companies fall into one of two camps. First, there's a small set of companies for whom new growth is not an immediate concern. Their current growth strategies remain robust, and they haven't yet exhausted the traditional growth moves. The majority of companies, however, have exhausted or will soon exhaust the growth potential of traditional moves. Their industries have already consolidated, international markets have largely been claimed, and product innovation has slowed. As a result, the core business is growing modestly or not at all.

Look in the mirror and ask, *Which of these categories does my company* **honestly** *fit into*? If you are lucky, you may still have opportunities to pursue traditional growth moves. But for most companies, pursuing new-growth opportunities should be the number-one priority.

Notice that most companies are moving along a time curve that inescapably carries growing businesses into a no-growth zone. Even the best-conceived business models run out of steam eventually. It's important to recognize how close you are to the inevitable slowdown. Ideally, you'll begin to seriously tackle the problem of new growth several years ahead of that point.

When things are still going well, you have the organizational energy and the financial resources to create new opportunities; Wall Street will grant you the freedom to move into new market spaces, and employees will tackle new challenges with confidence. Take advantage of these assets sooner rather than later—difficult though it may be to take aggressive action at a time when your prospects appear rosy and the temptations of complacency are powerful.

The great paradox of business is this: You should be most aggressive about creating new growth when the business model is at the *peak* of its performance—that is, at the moment when you least seem to need to, and when you are least psychologically prepared to do so.

How Great Is My Growth Gap?

Successful planning for growth begins with understanding the objective. You first need to decide on a realistic growth target.

Examine the growth assumptions your company or division has previously established. Ask, *What is our target annual growth rate? How much incremental revenue does this translate into every year? Given our current situation and the dynamics of our industry, is this a realistic target? Do we lead our competitors or lag behind them?*

Remember, as the Cardinal Health story illustrates, it's important to think in terms of both absolute and relative growth rates; both parameters help determine your own company's specific growth target. In addition, consider such relevant factors as employee and investor expectations, which are influenced in turn by your company's track record, industry norms, economic forecasts, and a host of intangibles.

Apply the best analysis of these elements to defining a realistic, sustainable set of growth targets for your company, including both revenue and profit growth for the next three to five years.

Next, look at the status of your current growth plans and activities. Start by listing the major growth initiatives currently in place or on the drawing board, along with your expectations about how much incremental revenue and profit each will provide over the next three years. Then go a little deeper and estimate the probability-adjusted expectation for growth from each initiative, combining the projected revenue from an initiative with your best estimate of the percentage chance of achieving that success.

Finally, do a bit of qualitative analysis of your current growth plans. Ask, *How will success in each of these initiatives affect my company or division more broadly? Will it enhance our strategic positioning? Will it build a bridge to further growth initiatives or simply protect the core business? Which of our current or proposed initiatives are incremental moves or modest extensions, and which have the potential to create breakthrough growth?*

The answers to these questions will help determine whether or not the current list of initiatives will enable you to meet your growth targets. Not every company is facing a major growth gap. If you are growing at 6 percent with a target of 8 percent, you may be able to squeeze a couple of percentage points from product innovation or some other traditional move. If you're like most companies, however, your current growth plans will probably fall short. Now we'll consider ways of closing that gap.

Where Do My Initiatives Fall Along the Growth Spectrum?

The analysis you've done so far already gives you a leg up on most competitors. Many companies make vague or high-level statements about growth. Only a few turn these statements into precise percentage and dollar targets. Even fewer map their growth targets back to specific initiatives to understand precisely where their growth will come from.

Growth moves fall along a spectrum of categories, ranging from Traditional to Information-Driven moves (as shown in figure 17-1).

Map your company's current and proposed growth initiatives across the rows of the growth spectrum. The resulting picture is often very revealing.

The moves listed in Row A—acquisitions, international growth, price increases, and cost cutting—have been the primary growth engines for most companies in the past two decades. They are still the preferred route in a few industries . . . but the opportunities are shrinking fast.

In some industries, where the technology is not fully mature, the moves in Row B may sustain growth for years to come. However, most companies that have *all* their growth moves concentrated in Rows A and B are running high-risk portfolios.

Figure 17-1.
The Growth Spectrum

A. Traditional	• International • Acquisitions • Price • Cost cutting
B. Enhanced Product Position	• New products • Extensions • Differentiation
C. Transitional	• Resegmentation • Replicate the best customer • Value-based pricing • Strategic customer program • Turning product offers into system offers • Etc.
D. New Growth	• Product/service integration • Bundled solutions • Value-added outsourcing • Downstream offers • Etc.
E. Information-Based	• Integrated information offering • Performance guarantees • Selling information • Externalizing IT investments • Etc.

The moves in Row C are customer-centric. They force the kind of economic learning that produces real short-term revenue increases and paves the way for success in Row D.

Row D represents new skills most companies are just beginning to learn. It includes the kind of growth moves that Cardinal, Johnson, Air Liquide, OnStar, and Deere have spent half a decade mastering— moves that focus on adding new value to the customer beyond product functionality.

Finally, Row E contains growth moves that monetize the information about customers, markets, and processes that have been developed over time. These moves have particularly attractive strategic characteristics: low asset intensity, difficult to imitate, and generating long-term competitive advantage.

Mapping your growth initiatives in this way can spark conversations about the effectiveness of your growth planning and the likelihood that your plans will succeed.

This exercise can help you determine how well the structure of your action plan aligns with the realities of your business and your industry. For example, suppose all of your initiatives are in Row A but you compete in an industry that is already fully consolidated and international. In that case, your plan isn't structurally sound. Similarly, if you're devoting all your energy to Rows D and E, yet your organization is not ready to implement these moves effectively, you are likely wasting valuable resources.

The growth spectrum is also a powerful tool for analyzing the balance of your company's growth investments. Most companies tend to overinvest in moves at the top of the spectrum, because these are the areas they are most familiar with and where they have well-established processes and systems to manage initiatives. Don't think of investment only in terms of money; also consider where your most thoughtful, energetic, and catalytic managers work. Are they all assigned to initiatives at the top, or are you leveraging their talents to deliver results at the bottom of the spectrum?

Make sure that you are at least exploring options in all five categories, so that you have a strong pipeline of future growth and of new skills and capabilities.

What Is My Growth Action Plan?

The challenge, then, is to build a comprehensive action plan that encompasses a sufficient number of nontraditional growth moves and properly allocates resources so that they are aligned with the areas offering the greatest growth potential. More than a laundry list of initiatives, the action plan should be a structured tool that will help ensure that you don't waste resources or let valuable opportunities pass by and that you are working to systematically reduce the risk of your growth moves. Perhaps most important, the process of developing the plan will be a catalyst for dialogue about the growth challenge and your company's readiness to meet it.

Use a template like the one in figure 17-2 to sketch out an action plan in one place.

The best action plans are constructed through an active, honest dialogue among senior managers, middle managers, and key customers. The shared objectives of the dialogue should be to clearly map all initiatives against an explicit growth goal; to consider *all* the potential growth initiatives in your company (including those buried and possibly under-resourced in the divisions); to drive resources to initiatives in a way that matches growth expectations; to realistically assess the hidden liabilities that will make growth harder and plan to overcome them; and to assign clear responsibility for each initiative to an individual or group accountable for results.

Crafting a growth plan that achieves these goals won't happen in a few hours or overnight. It takes energy, commitment, creativity, and openness from everyone on the leadership team. As the plan emerges (with contributions from many people, through many iterations, over a period of weeks or months), you'll want to examine and reexamine it repeatedly, considering such questions as:

1. **Is our growth plan aggressive enough to meet the organization's growth needs?** The plan should include a buffer against the unexpected (which, of course, should be the expected). If everything has to go 100 percent according to plan in order to meet your targets, either your targets are too aggressive or your plan is not aggressive enough.

Figure 17-2.
THE GROWTH ACTION PLAN TEMPLATE

	5-Year Growth Target: $_____			
	My Top Growth Moves	Expected share of revenue/ profit growth (Total adds to 100%)	Share of resource allocation (Total adds to 100%)	Major hidden liabilities to overcome
Traditional	• • •	_____%	_____%	• • •
Enhanced Product Position	• • •	_____%	_____%	• • •
Transitional	• • •	_____%	_____%	• • •
New Growth	• • •	_____%	_____%	• • •
Information-Based	• • •	_____%	_____%	• • •

2. **Is our plan practical? That is, is it capable of being implemented by our company within a reasonable time frame?** To answer this question, you need to consider such factors as your access to the necessary resources and skills; your mapping of available capital, people, and other resources against specific initiatives; and your awareness of the hidden liabilities associated with your targeted initiatives and your ability to overcome them.

3. **Is our plan realistic? Are we balancing our investments based on a sober assessment of where our growth opportunities lie?** In many cases, developing a comprehensive growth action plan will also involve creating an investment migration plan that over time shifts resources away from traditional growth moves and toward new growth and information-based moves. Such a migration plan provides a staged process during which you gain the resources, skills, and self-confidence necessary for new-growth initiatives to succeed.

Building a plan that represents a balanced attack on the growth challenge will help you avoid the peaks and valleys in which so many companies bog down. Instead of waiting for one set of moves to run out of steam before investigating next steps, you will be continually investigating and pursuing new-growth initiatives—constantly pushing your company forward.

Like any other form of business planning, building a growth plan involves both art and science. There will always be trade-offs that must be weighed in light of judgment and experience: between short- and long-term initiatives, low- and high-risk moves, traditional and nontraditional moves, and core and noncore opportunities.

Variations on a Theme

No two companies can expect to follow the same growth plan. Every industry has a unique set of opportunities and constraints; every firm has a unique pattern of hidden assets and liabilities to be leveraged and overcome. Just as smart investors develop personalized asset allocation plans that fit their age, income, investment goals, and risk tolerance, the smart management team develops a company-specific growth plan tailored to its special strengths and the challenges of its environment.

To illustrate, let's consider companies in a range of situations. Perhaps you'll recognize some parallels between these situations and your own.

"King Electronics" is one of today's large, successful technology companies for which there are few or no traditional growth moves left. King has already achieved a dominant position in its industry and has expanded internationally. There may be opportunities in enhanced product offerings, but these moves in and of themselves are not large enough to move the needle on growth. A growth action plan for King, therefore, might include 30 percent enhanced product moves, 30 percent transitional, and 40 percent new growth and information-based moves.

"Catalytic Industries" needs to focus even more heavily on the lower rows. Catalytic operates in a thoroughly consolidated and globalized industry that has not seen a major technical innovation in more than a decade. Thus, both traditional and enhanced product moves are likely to produce little future growth. Yet Catalytic's leadership is unfamiliar with new-growth thinking and the skills it requires. To avoid wasting resources on initiatives in Rows A and B, Catalytic should focus on transitional moves in the near term so as to build the capabilities required to execute the new growth and information-based moves it will need in the future. Catalytic's balance might look something like 70 percent transitional, 30 percent new growth and information-based.

Finally, "Expert Services" competes in an industry that looks like securities brokerage in the early to mid-1980s: fragmented, with only a small percentage of revenues drawn from international markets. Expert Services needs a plan that focuses in the near to medium term on traditional and enhanced product moves. At the same time, knowing that the end of these moves is in sight, the company should build capabilities and investigate opportunities in the lower rows. Perhaps its portfolio of moves should be 60 percent weighted in the first two rows, 40 percent in the remaining three.

The goal of developing an action plan is not to establish yet another strategic process to occupy senior managers' time with iteration after iteration of interesting ideas. Nor is it a budgeting process, where numbers and their accuracy is paramount. Instead, the goal is to create a comprehensive road map that managers can use as a tool to drive new growth in a comprehensive, balanced, structurally sound, implementable, and measured fashion. And the dialogue that the planning process generates—honest, challenging, creative, and continuous—is at least as important as any documents produced. As Dwight D. Eisenhower remarked about preparing for battle: "Plans are useless, but planning is indispensable."

The Acid Test

In the end, the success or failure of your growth action plan will depend on the support it receives from the most important constituents: your employees (especially those in the top 10 percent of performance), your board members (especially those who are most active and insightful), and your investors (especially those who are most tenacious and jaded).

Before deciding that the plan is ready to implement, step into the shoes of these three sets of stakeholders and ask yourself the questions they will ask.

1. **Employees** are betting their careers and much of their financial well-being on the company's growth prospects. Consciously or not, every day that they come to work (rather than searching for new jobs elsewhere) they are reaffirming their belief in the company's leadership and the soundness of its growth planning. If you hope to sustain

that belief, think about the answers to questions such as these:

- Does your growth plan make sense? What are the chances of your company implementing it— your company as it really is, with its underutilized hidden assets, its maddening hidden liabilities, and its deeply ingrained organizational strengths and weaknesses?
- What kind of investment is the company making in this plan? Does next year's budget actually reflect your self-proclaimed growth priorities? Will your CEO and other leading executives devote their own personal time to these initiatives?
- Where are the most promising, skilled, and ambitious managers in your company being sent? Do your growth initiatives get the necessary share of leadership attention and talent, or are they quietly being staffed with second-rate managers?
- Do you know why the last several growth efforts failed? What will the company do differently this time to ensure success?

2. **The members of the board** have become increasingly conscious in recent years of the responsibility they bear for the company's future. They know that if the firm stagnates because management failed to recognize and act upon new-growth opportunities, the board members will receive a share of the scrutiny and blame. To win

their support for your plan, be ready to respond to questions such as these:

- What has been the true quality of your growth over the past five to seven years? Have you created a lot of "bad growth" through channel stuffing, price cutting, profitless volume, et cetera? Going forward, how much can you count on continued product-based growth? How urgently do you need to create next-generation sources of growth?
- Is your current management team capable of pursuing demand innovation and new growth? What track record of growth and innovation has it established to date?
- Are you doing enough to motivate your employees to create growth? Does your compensation and organization system catalyze or kill new growth?
- How greatly are you constrained by external expectations including those of Wall Street? What is your plan for managing (and changing) these expectations?

3. **Investors** are probably feeling shell-shocked and defensive, given the continuing turbulence of financial markets. They are desperately seeking companies with *real* growth prospects, unsweetened by accounting gimmickry or blue-skies optimism. To enlist their support, be ready to answer questions like these:

- How realistic is your growth target for the next few years? Is it aligned with industry dynamics?

- What percentage of your current portfolio is mature revenue that isn't growing at all? How much growth does the rest of your portfolio have to generate to produce an attractive picture overall?

- How big is the gap between your target growth rate and the growth remaining in your current strategy?

- How does your growth plan map against the growth spectrum? Is the mix aggressive enough? Is it realistic?

- How aggressively are you investing to pursue your growth moves? Are you doing what it takes to acquire or develop the capabilities needed to grow, especially toward the bottom of the growth spectrum?

If you don't have solid answers to *all* these questions, then you don't have a great action plan for growth.

And here's one more tough truth: Constructing your action plan and answering these questions once is merely a good start, not the end of the process. Managing new growth needs to include an active feedback loop in which you are constantly monitoring the progress of each initiative, its changing probability of success, and its shifting risk profile. You can be learning from your successes and failures, looking for new opportunities, and assessing your resource allocation. Just as a personal investment portfolio benefits from asset allocation reviews—especially when the markets shift direction—your company's growth action plan will benefit from regular, tough-minded growth reviews. Think of the action plan template above all as a tool that you share with senior managers and other employees in order to stimulate an ongoing conversation about growth.

Creating a Little Growth Today Avoids a Lot of Problems Tomorrow

The good news is that if you begin the process *now,* you will probably be one or two steps ahead of most competitors. But don't wait. For most firms, the only real alternative to fostering a new-growth discipline is to be relegated to endless management challenges generated by stagnation.

In an age when P/E multiples have come back down to earth and many large companies have reduced costs as much as they can, creating real new growth will be an increasingly vital source of shareholder value. Large-scale stagnation has happened frequently in the past. Between 1969 and 1981, there was zero appreciation in the Dow. Between 1990 and 2001, there was zero appreciation in the Nikkei. Companies unwilling to face the hard task of growth risk the same fate in the coming decade on a painfully intimate scale.

You have the opportunity to avoid this fate. You have the opportunity to reenergize your management and your employees and develop a leadership position in creating growth for your industry. Now is the time to seize it.

18

Tools and Techniques
You Can Use Today:
Mercer's Demand
Innovation Website
(www.DemandInnovation.com)

On our website (www.DemandInnovation.com), you
will find tools, frameworks, and additional analyses to
begin applying demand innovation thinking in your
organization. Specific tools include:

- A diagnostic to help you evaluate your company's
  real growth situation.
- Worksheets to help sort through and identify high-
  potential growth opportunities that your company
  can pursue.
- Tools for identifying, cataloging, and evaluating
  the hidden assets inside your company.
- A process to help you assemble a balanced portfolio of growth moves tailored to your unique situation.

- Templates to help you identify the hidden liabilities that may torpedo your growth efforts and develop plans to mitigate them.

Also available is more detail on certain topics in this book, additional case studies, and points of view on how demand innovation is relevant to particular industries such as high-tech and pharmaceuticals.

We hope that the ideas in this book have energized you and have provided insight into how you can help create new growth in your company. It's up to *you* to make new growth happen.

Acknowledgments

Like our previous books, *How to Grow When Markets Don't* is the product of the organizational and intellectual energy that generates insights for the clients of Mercer Management Consulting. Experience gleaned from working closely with our clients prodded us to look beyond traditional tactics to explore the underlying dynamics that make growth such a challenge in today's environment. We owe thanks to those clients, for they have continued to push us to gain a deeper understanding of this next step in growth thinking. By asking tough questions, they have provided us with the opportunity to work with them as they confronted their most pressing strategic issue.

We thank Karl Weber, who contributed enormously to writing *How to Grow When Markets Don't*. In addition to sharing his own ideas and anecdotes, Karl's ability to communicate the concepts and potential of demand innovation via analyses, narratives, and his professional observations was crucial in presenting these important concepts to readers.

We also thank Rick Wolff at Warner Books for his coaching, encouragement, guidance, and feedback as the manuscript was developed. His insights helped to shape our approach and to find the right balance among framework, anecdotes, and ideas.

The entire Mercer team shared their research, ideas, and enthusiasm. Without the support of Peter Coster, president of Mercer Inc., David Morrison, president of Mercer Management Consulting, and Jim Down, former vice-chairman of the firm, we never could have collected the organization's ideas and insights nor integrated them into a useful framework and manuscript. Our Mercer partners, including Charlie Hoban, Ted Moser, Hanna Moukanas, and Bill Stevenson, also contributed their diverse industry experience to validate and improve many of the concepts we have created.

Mercer's Marketing Group, including Pat Pollino, John Campbell, Nancy Lotane, and Ellen Zanino, provided important help in shaping our message and helping refine many aspects of the book. Thanks as well to Ruth Mills, Hilary Hinzmann, and Jeff Wise, whose editorial support helped enhance the message.

A special thank-you goes to the *How to Grow When Markets Don't* research team, led by Andy Johnston and Tine Christensen and including Amina Belghiti, Sean Farrell, Steve Won, Brian Rixner, Jag Duggal, and Chris Kemmitt. They gathered much of the research material and shaped many of the concepts included in the book. Their insights and energy were critical to propelling this project from start to finish.

Adrian Slywotzky
Richard Wise

Lexington, Massachusetts
September 2002

Index